# Philip Johnson

MAKERS OF CONTEMPORARY ARCHITECTURE
R. Buckminster Fuller by John McHale
Philip Johnson by John M. Jacobus, Jr.
Louis I. Kahn by Vincent Scully, Jr.
Eero Saarinen by Allan Temko
Kenzo Tange by Robin Boyd

MASTERS OF WORLD ARCHITECTURE
Alvar Aalto by Frederick Gutheim
Antonio Gaudí by George R. Collins
Walter Gropius by James Marston Fitch
Le Corbusier by Françoise Choay
Eric Mendelsohn by Wolf Von Eckardt
Ludwig Mies van der Rohe by Arthur Drexler
Pier Luigi Nervi by Ada Louise Huxtable
Richard Neutra by Esther McCoy
Oscar Niemeyer by Stamo Papadaki
Louis Sullivan by Albert Bush-Brown
Frank Lloyd Wright by Vincent Scully, Jr.

# Philip Johnson
## by John M. Jacobus, Jr.

George Braziller  New York  1962

*For information address the publisher,*
*George Braziller, Inc.*
*215 Park Avenue South*
*New York 3, New York*

*Library of Congress Catalog Card Number: 62–16264*

*Printed in the United States of America*

*First Printing*

*The selection from "The Current Work of*
*Philip Johnson," by Henry-Russell Hitchcock,*
*is reprinted from Zodiac, VIII, 1961,*
*with the kind permission*
*of the editors and the author.*

# Acknowledgment

This account of the architecture
of Philip Johnson is presented
as an interim report. It has been my
intention to give a representative
picture of his work, but I have not
sought to be either exhaustive or
definitive. This presentation would
be unthinkable in its present form
without the interest and cooperation
of the architect himself, and the help
rendered by his staff. The alert reader
will be aware of my dependence
upon Mr. Johnson's own writings
concerning his work as well as
contemporary architecture in general,
and of my great indebtedness to
the perceptive commentaries of
Professor Henry-Russell Hitchcock
on these same subjects. It is nearly
impossible to render adequate
homage to these pioneers in the
history of Modern Architecture.
This book has been substantially
enriched through the inclusion of
excerpts from Mr. Johnson's writings
relating to the contemporary architectural
situation. Mr. Johnson has very
graciously allowed me to make this
selection; hence, the responsibility
for possible omissions is mine.
I am indebted to Miss Marie-Anne
Middeleer of Mr. Johnson's staff
who greatly facilitated the
gathering of photographs for this
volume, to Miss Ellen Weiss who helped
with the initial research, and to
Miss Sandra Ward who typed the final draft
and improved its style in countless ways.

JOHN M. JACOBUS, JR.
*University of California, Berkeley*

*For Dan and Wilma*

# Contents

*Text*  11

*Notes to the Text*  44

*Chronology*  46

*Plates*  49

*Selected Writings of Philip Johnson*  113

*Bibliography*  123

*Index*  125

*Illustration Credits*  128

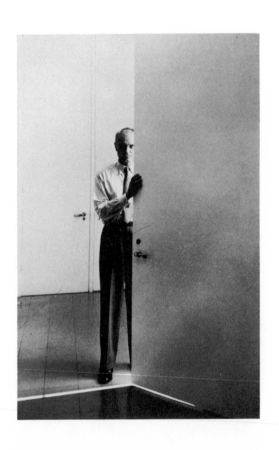

In the evolution of 20th-century architecture, Philip Johnson has played a unique dual role. He began as a critic and historian of architecture and in this capacity he was associated with the original formulation of the concept "International Style" as applied to the new architecture of the 1920's.[1] The intelligence and taste which first contributed to this fundamental statement concerning modern design are likewise determining factors in Johnson's more recent creative activity. As an artist, he has displayed in his own buildings the same incisive analytical traits that first found expression in his architectural writings thirty years ago. Indeed, this literary relationship between his personal manner of design, which was established about 1950, and the geometric simplicity of the radical architecture of a generation ago, not only reveals the sources of his style but also explains the scholarly nature of his preoccupation with these archetypal modern constructions. Furthermore, Johnson is a traditionalist by necessity as well as by choice and temperament. Born in 1906, he is a full generation younger than the leading creative architects of the 1920's, most of whom were born in the mid-1880's. This simple matter of chronology helps to explain the inherently retrospective character of his creative work—retrospective in spite of his forthright adoption of a radical design vocabulary, one which was originally drawn from the style of Mies van der Rohe. Johnson's place in contemporary history is dramatized by the fact that he was still an undergraduate in Harvard College at a time when a major landmark of the new style, Walter Gropius' Bauhaus, of 1925–26, was under construction. The paths of their respective careers were to cross only later, when Johnson returned to Harvard as an architectural student in the early 1940's, shortly after the self-exiled German architect had become the chairman of its Department of Architecture.

During the first half of the 20th century, a vocal and even brazen individuality was a fundamental qualification for the artist or architect, whose very modernity frequently depended upon the violence of his clash with established values of tradition and practice. Even at mid-century, this view of creativity is still widely recognized. The iconoclastic attitude of the International Style architects with respect to historical forms, together with their fondness for severe, uncompromisingly plain designs, provided much more than the mere illusion of novelty or the suggestion of gratuitous revolution. This new

12  architecture of the 1920's responded to that period's passionate and idealistically motivated craving for the creation of fresh themes and ideas that could contribute to a liberated, extroverted artistic expression. *Purism* in France, *de Stijl* in Holland, *Futurism* in Italy, the *Bauhaus* in Germany and *Constructivism* in Russia were only local tags or labels for the specific, individual manifestations of this phenomenon, which eventually was recognized as a broad, truly international movement dedicated to the renovation of architecture. Equally, these new developments in building design played an integral role in the general re-evaluation and upheaval that was taking place in the art, music, and literature of the day. The various personalities—Le Corbusier and André Lurçat in France, J. J. P. Oud and Gerrit Rietveld in Holland, Walter Gropius and Ludwig Mies van der Rohe in Germany—gradually revealed an individual identity in their works, and at the same time manifested an apparently common aim and solidarity in the simple, clear forms that their work affected at that time.

The formal baptism of the International Style, in 1932, accomplished in the title of a book by Henry-Russell Hitchcock and Philip Johnson, was a harbinger of certain fundamental, if not immediately visible, changes of attitude. Having reached the point at which it could be historically identified and defined, the new architecture had simultaneously passed its point of maximum creativity, and in certain ways its forms and ideals rapidly began to lose urgency and immediacy. After 1930 the unitary spirit and force of contemporary architecture were dissipated in a number of directions. Individual architects began a search for more personal modes of expression. The less gifted and determined architects of the 1920's turned to more conventional patterns of design, while the major figures, Le Corbusier, Gropius, and Mies van der Rohe, sought to explore more intensively some special feature of the common style. As in all truly creative activity, the later works of these subsequently lauded masters resulted in the destruction and elimination of certain characteristics of the original International Style, and the introduction of seemingly new themes. Nonetheless, this process of creative destruction necessarily entailed the rebirth of many compositional elements familiar in the best post-World War I architecture, although frequently cloaked in a new and unfamiliar guise.

In the 1930's new personalities emerged who both modified

and enriched the ardently severe style of the previous decade.
Gropius found a disciple and sometime collaborator in Marcel
Breuer, a Bauhaus pupil; certain features of Le Corbusier's
manner were emulated by a group of Brazilian architects,
notably Lúcio Costa, Oscar Niemeyer, and Affonso Eduardo
Reidy; and the vernacular of the International Style was
introduced to the United States by the Viennese-educated Rudolph Schindler and Richard Neutra, along with the once-
proper Philadelphian, George Howe. Philip Johnson is a
contemporary of certain of these second-generation designers
in a spiritual as well as in a purely chronological way, although his career as an active builder did not begin until
later, in the 1940's. Consequently his style has developed in
a period which has seen the emergence of yet another group
of architects: Eero Saarinen, Paul Rudolph, and Minoru
Yamasaki. This third, most recent, group has broken in a
much more distinct way with the unique heritage of the International Style than had the earlier group of followers of which
Johnson is a spiritual member. In one sense, that of holding
an ambiguous or unclear historical position between the first
and second generation of post-International Style designers,
the only contemporary architect who can be convincingly
bracketed with Johnson is Louis I. Kahn.

Five years Johnson's senior, Kahn really did not begin to
show uniqueness and individuality in his work until the early
1950's, that is to say, just after Johnson's particular position
had been established with the construction of the Glass House
in 1949. While their works and principles would seem outwardly to have very little in common, both of these late-bloom-
ing architects seem to represent a continuation of one aspect
or another of early 20th-century modernism, in contrast to the
ostensibly negative attitude toward the recent past that is
adopted by certain of their contemporaries. Johnson has
tended to explore the formalistic, even stylish aspects of the
International Style heritage in his buildings of the 1950's,
whereas Kahn appears to have pursued its rational ideology in
a patient, deliberate way, with the result that he has at last
wrested a series of new, individual forms out of the older,
seemingly exhausted methodology. In effect the works of both
have a quality of persistence and fulfillment, and hence
parallel the later work of such International Style veterans as
Mies and Le Corbusier, especially in those designs where the

14  older architects develop and exploit themes that occurred in their own work a quarter-century before.

A part of this development in the general expansion of 20th-century architecture, begun in the 1930's but not brought to culmination until the 1950's, has proceeded by means of introspection and self-criticism. In addition, the architecture of this period has been confronted with a series of reactions of varying intensities. First came the ruthless suppression of the new style in Russia and Germany in the early 1930's. Other more basic inroads were made in the solid front of architectural modernism in the late 1930's and 1940's. *New Empiricism* in Scandinavia, the *Bay Region Style* on the Pacific coast of the United States, and the *neo-Picturesque* aesthetic supported by the influential English magazine, *The Architectural Review*, were all elements that indicated a gradual yet powerful transformation of taste at this time; and these phenomena would seem to mark the end of the original International Style movement. Even a Bauhaus-trained architect like Marcel Breuer, while not an active participant in these "organic" movements, nonetheless manifests similar tendencies in his domestic architecture of the 1940's. Architectural form became less incisive than in the 1920's, and a superficial romanticism seems to have vitiated the forthright geometrical purism of the previous period.

Toward the end of the 1940's, there was a resurgence of activity on the part of the International Style veterans, especially Mies and Le Corbusier, each of whom had quietly sought and discovered a new mode of expression. Both architects built upon principles of the International Style, but simultaneously were able to transcend its limitations. It is in the context of this resurgent modernism that the work of Philip Johnson must be situated. The key monuments in which the new architectural metamorphosis was indelibly crystallized were Mies's several buildings of the 1940's and '50's for the Illinois Institute of Technology, Chicago, and Le Corbusier's vast apartment block, the *Unité d'Habitation*, Marseilles, 1946–52. The former represented a pristine, simplified and regularized restatement of the delicately balanced but more dynamic and fluid spaces of the old International Style, whereas Le Corbusier's "new" mode resulted from a strategic and fertile balance between an impulsive, sculpturesque formalism and the discipline of a regularizing proportional system known as the Modulor. Both architects had attained

an ultimate, apotheosized creative maturity by 1950, one
that reached even beyond their brilliant achievements of the
late 1920's. To bring about this new burst of imaginative yet
disciplined architectural invention in the 1940's and early
1950's, a high degree of introspection and a willingness to
sacrifice at least the outward forms of the earlier styles were
absolutely necessary. In this respect, the recent work of Mies
and Le Corbusier remains more inventive than traditional,
even though their respective new manners have helped to
engender a new traditionalism. Since Philip Johnson is a
junior participant in this movement, it is especially appropriate that he is a biographer and interpreter of Mies van der
Rohe.[2] Johnson is also the practicing architect who, more than
anyone else, has transformed the personal style of the great
German-born Mies into a vernacular style—one that possesses
distinctively American as well as international implications.
In this process, the Miesian idiom was converted into a less
personal manner which subsequently could be employed as a
kind of tradition by the architectural profession as a whole.
Johnson's reduction and generalization of Mies's formal vocabulary tended to suppress certain structural implications
of the original; and through this simplification, the younger
architect helped to make the style readily communicable to
lesser designers. That many of today's derivative architects
have vulgarized the initial intentions of Mies and his disciple
is much to be regretted; yet it would be unjust to hold the
creators responsible for the shortcomings of their imitators.

At the same time, to consider Johnson's early work as exclusively Miesian in spirit is as gross an error as to assume
that his more monumental work of the last three or four years
is anti-Miesian. Johnson was most certainly never satisfied
with exclusively 20th-century source material, and from the
design of the Glass House in the late forties onward there are
veiled indications in the buildings themselves that he was
going directly to many of the same Romantic-Classic sources
of about 1800 to which Mies had turned in the early 20th
century. Toward the end of the 1950's, these aspects of his
inspiration became more and more apparent in the surfaces
of his designs, but it would be a mistake to interpret this shift
in emphasis as a total revolution in Johnson's architecture.
Indeed, the continuity and patient, sequential development of
his work from the late 1940's to the early 1960's can be seen
in the gradual evolution of his unique and expressive spatial

16 concepts. It was the development of a more vivid spatial articulation in the 1956 Boissonnas House, and the subsequent emergence of traditional, visually isolated interior spaces in the Munson-Williams-Proctor Institute, that engendered a more massive, tactile vocabulary in his design of enclosing walls and piers.

Clearly, Johnson is not primarily a pioneer or explorer. He is, instead, an architect whose work mirrors, clarifies, and expands accomplishments of the recent, still relevant past—a past which in many respects seems to have been more intensely creative and alive to new possibilities and opportunities than much tentative work of the immediate present. If Johnson's work from the 1940's through the late 1950's has been part of the avant-garde, it is equally a body of work characteristic of a transitional period. It tends to round out the achievement of the immediate past, filling in a few blank spaces that were left unrealized in the course of a more feverish leap forward. However, at the same time it seems neither to suggest a clearly identifiable path of new development, nor to predict future growth. This observation is advanced dispassionately, with the understanding that a sudden shift or change in emphasis may abruptly render the judgment erroneous or irrelevant. It is further recognized that the development of modern architecture as a whole has, in the early 1960's, reached a state of congestion and immobility. This is as true of the seemingly improvised forms of Kahn, Saarinen, or Rudolph as it is of the terse, disciplined, and more frankly academic modern style of Johnson. Consequently, Johnson's buildings manifest certain unresolved problems that have contributed to the current slackening of modern architecture's stylistic and philosophic growth. If Johnson's work is academic in spirit, he is no less a modernist because of it. The acceptance of this paradox is mandatory to a sensible appreciation of today's characteristic architecture, whether highly personal or anonymous.

One of the reasons for the problematic, hesitant character of much contemporary architecture is that the avant-garde has, in part, lost its reason for being. By now, it has absorbed those aspects of architectural convention and tradition which had not been routed by the general shift in popular taste after World War II. In one way or another, nearly every present-day architect, whatever his station or real sentiment, at least professes allegiance to the outward materialistic manifestations of the creative revolution that took place with the International Style. Our mid-century pattern not only makes it difficult to distinguish the hero from the villain; it deprives architects, especially the younger ones, of a militant sense of objectives upon which they can focus their efforts. Whatever were the failings of the functionalist and anti-traditionalist slogans of the early 20th century, they were important as easily comprehensible gestures which communicated a spirit of enthusiasm and determination rather than any deep-seated theory or philosophy. Johnson's generation has tended to demand too much in the way of intellectual substance from these old battle cries possibly because, as a group, it has failed to re-examine the total historical situation which accompanied the rise of the modern architectural style. Consequently, architects today have become indifferent to those aims of the heroic period which now seem to be a trifle naïve in their missionary zeal.

By the same token, there is an original, if not overtly novel, character to every Johnson design: a personal quality which in both basic concept and realization sets his buildings apart from those of his predecessors. Even though his work began by being heavily and profoundly indebted to the middle and late styles of Mies van der Rohe, and even though this quality persisted until his designs of the mid-1950's (ironically just at the time that he became Mies's collaborator in the design of the Seagram Building),[3] there was a fundamental difference of approach which changed essentials of spatial and psychic impact rather than incidentals of design. Mies's pure forms resulted from a long, determined struggle to achieve simplicity and precision. Johnson's come about from a calculated decision to adopt Mies's already existent manner, and to use it for somewhat different purposes. Thus, with Mies, the external skin of a building shares an equal importance with the spaces that it encloses. Johnson, on the other hand, has frequently upset this balance, so that the spaces, their scale and their interrelationships, assume priority over the neutral surfaces that enclose and define them.

In exploiting an assumed modernist style, Johnson had implicitly indicated that he was working in a tradition-oriented fashion, not far removed from that of the late Baroque 18th-century European architects. Before the onslaught of Revivalism and Eclecticism, these generations were the last to enjoy the benefits of designing within the frame of an in-

18    herited, limited, largely codified technique with respect both
to over-all composition and to individual detailing. Indeed,
there is a hermetic, epigrammatic quality latent in the designs
of Johnson that evokes—quite unconsciously, it would seem
—the century of Burlington, Kent, and Gabriel. His are buildings which come at the end, not at the beginning, of a particular historical phase; and in this respect Johnson is proved
to be an even more committed traditionalist than he himself
believes.

Johnson has assumed a dual role as both creator and critic
and, in doing so, has integrated action and contemplation.
The mid-20th century has become an age in which criticism is
not only practiced as an art but, furthermore, is practiced even
at the expense of more purely creative activity. Consequently,
Johnson is as much the representative as he is the spokesman
of his age. In each of his buildings one senses the application
of a critical and evaluative intelligence rather than the inventions of an inductive creative imagination.[4] With Mies, a
building's style and final form are the ultimate consequences
of a conceptual, rational process, but with Johnson the final
form of a building is the outgrowth of an arbitrary, pre-
established taste. Because of this, certain of his constructions
contain, implicitly, a series of critical comments and perhaps
even value judgments concerning their relevant prototypes.

It has been proposed that, in the last decade, the subject of
modern art has become, in a curiously narcissistic fashion,
modern art itself; that each significant contribution being
made today to the mainstream of contemporary art is a gloss
or commentary upon one or another aspect of the modernism
of the early 20th century.[5] Surely this comment is equally
relevant to architecture in the 1950's, and can be seen not just
in the work of Johnson, but also, less forcefully, in the creations of architects as dissimilar as Eero Saarinen, Paul
Rudolph, Louis Kahn, and Edward Stone, to name but a few.
Indeed, this evaluative, critical quality is even present in the
ultimate designs produced by Frank Lloyd Wright during the
last decade of his life. This is remarkable because the intui-
tive, spontaneous nature of Wright's inspiration would seem
a world removed from the calculated restraint of Johnson's
work. Nevertheless, in such works as the Guggenheim Museum
and the Marin County Center, Wright seems subconsciously
to have created memory-laden forms that look to the future in
their disregard for conventional or contemporary architectural

realities and, at the same time, seem to bear a far-reaching
message concerning the interpretation and reinterpretation of
the modern tradition.[6] In this respect Wright was intuitively
injecting a critical commentary into his final creations,
whereas Johnson was willfully and deliberately providing
this element as a major rather than a secondary element in
his designs.

In these various ways, the modern architecture of Philip
Johnson is distinguishable from that of his older contemporaries while, at the same time, it remains faithful to many of
their accomplishments. There is another controlling factor,
however, which provides a further contrast of Johnson's more
deliberate and self-conscious manner with that of the heroic
early modernists. This pertains to the distinctively American
quality in his work. Despite its well-advertised revolutionary
attitudes, 20th-century architecture, as a stylistic phenomenon,
is an organic outgrowth of the western European tradition.
Nevertheless, it is clear that the greatest creative figures who
represent the immediate, if indirect, ancestry of the new style
were Americans: Henry Hobson Richardson (1838–86),
Louis Sullivan (1856–1924), and Frank Lloyd Wright
(1869–1959). In turn, each of these men owed a great debt
to the academic and picturesque traditions of 19th-century
European eclecticism—indeed, their highly individual contributions are unthinkable without this background—and, at
the same time, each owed something of his originality to the
distance and separation from European centers afforded by
his American situation. Each of these men was able to gain
a dispassionate perspective of the continuing evolution of the
European tradition. Thus, they were simultaneously a part
of the continental tradition and separate from it. As Europeans
they were participants; as Americans they were spectators of
this evolutionary process. In effect, the center of development
of modern architecture remained in Europe during the late
19th and early 20th centuries. But the creative potential of
the distant, formerly colonial areas was becoming apparent
just when the older regions were beginning to show indications
of creative exhaustion. Although there were certainly consequential and inventive architects at work in Europe—men who
made useful contributions to the subsequent and more sharply
focused achievement of the International Style—none of them

quite touched the level sustained by these three American architects in their mature works.

The subsequent wave of creative activity in European architecture in the 1920's was in considerable measure influenced by the impact of this vital American architecture, especially through the widely admired works of Wright's early maturity, the years 1900–09. For a period from 1910 to about 1935 it seemed as if Wright's accomplishments had relevance only for the new European architecture, and their native American character was largely lost on the contemporary generation of American architects who were closely following established academic styles. Only later was the indigenous quality of Wright's work "discovered" by a new generation of American admirers, some of whom were looking for a native style with which to counteract the presumedly alien modernism of Europe. A valid interpretation of Wright's accomplishments must recognize that European and American elements are constantly intertwined at every stage in his development.

Because of this continuing sequence of parallels and interchanges, it is both useful and necessary to recognize distinctions between the two transatlantic cultural expressions. Far from being merely "provincial European," American art and architecture has had its own unique vision from the earliest colonial days of the 17th century. In it there is a sense of removal, of independence, and of distance. To overcome the inherent shortcomings of this situation, successive waves of American artists and writers chose to become expatriates. Consequently, there was a constant renewal and reintegration of American modes of expression through direct contact with the older, if now somewhat fallow, creative centers of Europe. It was more difficult for architects to use this safety valve, except in a limited way during student days. Nonetheless, Richardson, Sullivan, and Wright were spiritual expatriates, linking American with European architecture in a reciprocal exchange.

In a similar fashion, it was the geographical distance of critics like Hitchcock and Johnson that made it possible for them to perceive the nature of the International Style, and to realize that its importance was largely as a style, not merely as the manifestation of certain materialistic, functionalistic, and socio-economic doctrines. As a critic in the late 1920's and early 1930's, Johnson found it necessary to go to Europe, literally as well as figuratively, to find the new architecture.

Within a decade, by the time he resolved to become an architect, Europe had, in a sense, come to America. This occurred
most literally through the physical presence of Walter
Gropius, who became Professor of Architecture in the Graduate School of Design at Harvard in 1937 (becoming chairman
the following year), and Mies van der Rohe, who took charge
of the architectural program at Armour Institute, Chicago
(subsequently Illinois Institute of Technology), in 1938. In
this fashion the creative center of architectural gravity began
its shift from Europe to America, a process hastened by the
disturbing effects of World War II, and climaxed by the opportunities offered to American architects in the postwar
years. Since 1945 activity in the traditional European centers
has gradually subsided to the level one would expect to find
in quiet provincial capitals. Despite an intensified western
European building program which gained momentum in the
early 1960's, contemporary European architecture remains
stylistically and conceptually indebted to recent American
work, primarily of a commercial nature. Consequently, the
most recent phase of modern architectural growth, even in
Europe itself, has been expressly American in every respect;
whereas one or two generations ago the geographical and
ethnic balance was quite the reverse.

Looking historically at the architectural scene of the last
few years, we can interpret the recent work of Johnson, Kahn,
and even of Wright as an exemplary regional culmination of
late-19th- and early-20th-century European modes. Simultaneously, their work represents in varied, but equally valid,
ways the fulfillment of a specifically American architectural
heritage. The work of Philip Johnson must be evaluated in
terms of both the interlocking nature of this American-Euro-
pean relationship, and the subsequently overturned balance of
power which reached a culmination at about the time his own
style achieved maturity and distinctiveness. Johnson's work
exhibits a sense of detachment as well as of participation in
the European tradition—an ambiguous relationship similar
to that enjoyed by other distinguished American architects of
the recent past. In these several ways Johnson's works mark
a significant step in the development of mid-20th-century
architecture on an American as well as on an international
level. Conversely, when viewed in a different perspective, it is
even comprehensible as a specific event in the development

of a local, regional, New England style in the mid-20th century!

The particular refinements of concept and form, first treated with elegant clarity and subdued originality in Johnson's 1949 Glass House (plates 5–13, 15–17), are derived from certain innovations of the International Style, and are carried to their logical extreme with an almost hypnotic concentration. While the beginning of Johnson's "glass box" manner coincides with a broad public acceptance of this architectural idiom for commercial purposes (after several decades of contempt and ridicule), his style is unabashedly aristocratic rather than popular. Traditionally oriented in destination and service, his work sharply contrasts with that of his mentors, whose similar designs were the result of a more spirited, revolutionary attitude. Without doubt, Mies van der Rohe is the architect of the earlier 20th century with whom Johnson has the most in common. Unfortunately, this observation has become a truism so overworked that the younger architect's unique personal inclinations have been obscured. This is especially true of his historical curiosity which led him to explore independently certain 19th-century antecedents of 20th-century architecture, antecedents which had fascinated Mies himself years earlier. Unlike most contemporary architects of the older generation, Johnson makes no effort to hide his sources, but instead is proud and eager to reveal them. His architecture thereby gains meaning and expressive significance through its specific citation of recent historical precedent.[7]

Johnson has, for example, pointed out certain prototypes for the design of his epochal Glass House of 1949.[8] These are confined to sources contained either within the modern style of the early 20th century (Le Corbusier, van Doesburg, Malevitch, and Mies), or within the expressive, fashionable style of 1800, Romantic Classicism (the unexpected geometric inventiveness of Ledoux or the ingenious planning and siting subtleties of Schinkel). All of these influences have consciously been brought into play in the designing of Johnson's houses of the early and middle 1950's. Repeated inspiration from these myriad sources has not produced a series of extracts set off in quotation marks, but instead has created a style consistent in its evolution from one design to the next. The exploration of the steel-framed glass-box theme and its

relation to a real or imaginary stylobate in his own house of
1949 (plates 5–13, 15–17), the Ball House of 1953 (plate
33), the Wiley House of 1953 (plates 34–37), the Leonhardt
House of 1956 (plates 50–54), and its ultimate transformation within a more conventional brick pier structural system
in the design for the Boissonnas House of 1956 (plates
58–62), is a most obvious instance of his painstaking, almost
cautious, sequential development. In this respect, Johnson's
work possesses an organic unity, and each work thereby is
infinitely more than the sum of several influences. Perhaps
the term for it is creative criticism.

In actuality, while these conscious influences are the most
immediately noticeable features of his buildings, they ultimately prove to have affected little more than the letter of
the design. The spirit that informs his designs, and provides
them with their distinctive personal inflection, reaches back
to the sheltered, inviolate aristocratic world of the *ancien
régime*. Literally as well as figuratively they are pre-Revolu-
tionary. The tumult and conflict implicit in all architecture
since the 1780's, whether determined by historical prototypes
of form or by invention and cultivated originality of composition, are absent. The resourcefulness characteristic of revivalist and eclectic architecture and the spirited drive typical of new architectural movements during the first half of this
century are in sharp contrast with the tranquillity and detachment of Johnson's buildings. In this respect his impersonal,
frequently understated idiom has found especially fitting fulfillment recently in the design of museum structures in Utica,
New York (plates 72, 74, 76–83); Fort Worth, Texas (plates
84–88); and Lincoln, Nebraska (plates 90, 91). This fondness for understatement is characteristic of his work, at least
until the late 1950's. The emergence of a more overtly expressive monumental style in the Israel Nuclear Reactor
(plates 108–112) has implications that go beyond the suc-
cinctly clarified Miesian style and its motto of "Less Is More,"
which is Johnson's purported point of departure.

An explanation of this as well as of similar relationships
can best be made completely clear through detailed compari-
sons of individual buildings by master and disciple. In this
connection the historical contacts between the conception and
design of Mies's Farnsworth House, Plano, Illinois (plate 14),
projected in 1946 but not executed until 1951, and the almost
contemporary Glass House (plates 5–13, 15–17) might be

24 regarded as the architectural equivalent of a controlled laboratory experiment. Although the Mies "cottage" was the first to be designed, and hence provided the impetus for Johnson's own residence, it was not finished until after the completion of its equally famous progeny. Taken together, these two radical domestic designs represent one notable and extreme outgrowth of the by-then traditional International Style. Both must be regarded as extreme because of the uncompromising fashion in which the glass-wall concept was applied on all four sides of the volume to be "enclosed."

The use of glazed walls to create new kinds of visual, spatial, and textural effects is of course one of the abiding contributions of the International Style. The alternating effects of transparency and reflection, and the ensuing ambiguities of formal and spatial relationship which this material made feasible were, however, usually employed by the architects of the 1920's in conjunction with smooth, opaque stucco surfaces. This was done in part to gain a contrast and variety which would complement the vigorously articulated types of massing that were also popular at this time, frequently under the name of "functional" expression. Such pioneering constructions as Gropius' Bauhaus, Dessau, 1925–26, had employed an exterior envelope in which a thin-skinned opaque surface was contrasted with a generous use of glass, a combination which had the effect of largely but not completely destroying the palpability of the architectonic volume, as well as of partially negating the normal idea of enclosure. Similarly, Mies's lyrical Barcelona Pavilion of 1929 produced even more bewildering and ambiguous effects by the irregular positioning of polished marble slabs both to complement and contrast with the equally crystalline yet transparent surfaces of "enclosing" glass. These characteristic buildings of the late 1920's were almost inevitably irregular in shape, and they never went so far as to reduce the exterior envelope of the entire building to glass. This attainment was reserved for the architecture of the 1940's and 1950's.

In the Miesian idiom of the 1940's and in its Johnsonian development, variety and articulation in the buildings' mass were replaced by a determined regularity and cubic simplicity of outward form. Consonant with this refinement was the adoption of glass as an over-all enclosing material, so that a building contained no opaque external wall whatsoever. Despite the pioneer work of the twenties in the actual technique of

individual glazed walls, no building of that heroic period had
gone to such an ideologically pure, unadulterated extreme of
confounding the visual and spatial concepts of interior and
exterior. In this respect Mies's Farnsworth House and Johnson's Glass House represent both a logical and an illogical
extreme growing out of the International Style. While they
might seem to be the ultimate works of this severe and exacting
modernist idiom, in reality they can be characterized more
aptly as a kind of neo-International Style. They are buildings
which reassert some (but certainly not all) of the unique
values of the earlier architecture of the 1920's in a forced,
extreme, and somewhat artificial manner. The Farnsworth
House has a certain authentic, constructive rationale surviving
as a reflexive habit in the work of the veteran designer Mies.
The Glass House, on the other hand, bears all the hallmarks
of an architect who had watched and observed, but not par-
ticipated in, the original International Style and who, after
serious deliberation and reflection, set down his own comments. In this sense the Glass House is not an International
Style building, but rather a historical and critical exegesis
upon that style, infused with an air of objective detachment
that only a quarter-century's distance can provide.

The role of the Farnsworth House should concern us in
other respects, since it was the vehicle by which Johnson's
personal style was integrated into the new modernist tradition.
In 1947, at the beginning of the three-year period which led
to the design of his own Glass Pavilion, Johnson wrote of the
then-as-yet-unbuilt Farnsworth design that it was "conceived
as a floating, self-contained cage."[9] He went on to observe
that this was a radical departure from Mies's last European
domestic designs, the "earth-hugging court-houses" in which
the interior living spaces are oriented about a secluded, walled
court that is, in effect, an open-air living room. Significantly,
these projects dating from about 1931 to 1935 never reached
the stage of actual construction and it was Johnson who, with
his Cambridge, Massachusetts, residence of 1942 (plates 1,
2), actually built this Miesian type for the first time.[10]

In his own New Canaan house of 1949, Johnson avoided the
floating effect of the Farnsworth House, with its slablike stylobate elevated above the untended ground, as well as the dis-
crete structural expression inherent in Mies's white-painted
steel-frame design. Instead of concentrating upon an elegantly
conceived and provocative juncture between the horizontal and

26  vertical elements of the frame, a conception which in the Farnsworth House involves the expressive projection of the slabs of roof and stylobate beyond the points of vertical support, Johnson has provided a black steel frame that is more self-effacing than expressive of structure (compare plates 14 and 15). Johnson's less striking structural frame provides, paradoxically, the visual framework for a series of spatial experiences of greater subtlety and complexity. In effect, the Glass House is not a house but a monumentally scaled multi-purpose space set gently, but directly, upon the carefully tended green carpet of lawn, "sealed," but not separate, from its surroundings. When viewed from the inside, its already generously proportioned space expands outward, embracing the parklike setting, stopping only at the impenetrable façade of the solid brick-faced Guest House. The Guest House forms a significant tactile counterpart to the crystalline, transparent cube of the main house.

In a complementary fashion, when viewed from the exterior under certain lighting conditions (plate 5), the glass cube seems to dissolve, leaving the landscaped setting nearly intact and undisturbed. The contrasting cylinder of brick, however, remains as the only solid, tactile intrusion. Alternately, under other circumstances (plate 13), the black-framed glass becomes a mirror of its surroundings, providing a second means of clouding or camouflaging the actual form of the "house" or "room." Other qualities of the Glass House have been touched upon with insight by Henry-Russell Hitchcock, and the aptness of his observations merits repetition here:

One aspect of the Johnson house in use has no analogue in the Farnsworth house. For nearly six months of the year the living space in daytime is not the interior, but the surrounding grassed terrace to which the glass walls of the house provide only a backdrop, its outer definition being the low granite rail below which the ground drops off to the valley below and the wooded hills beyond. The Farnsworth house on the other hand is a sort of "beached yacht," with no provision for outdoor living beyond the very confined space of the fly-screened "deck" and the small open Travertine "dock" below it. A further related difference is that the waxed brick floor of the Johnson house is but a step above the level of the terrace to which the four doors give ready access. Moreover, the axially placed frames of these doors give an order to the metal frame of the glass box which some have called (with considerable exaggeration) Palladian. Mies may be "Classical" in spirit, but he has never been *cinquecento*. It is here, in two aspects that to some extent at least affect the spatial impression, that the subtle historicism of Johnson first appeared, both in the return to axial symmetry, toward which Mies himself had, of course, been moving by fits and starts ever since his Reichsbank project of 1933, and in the retention of a Wrightian sort of "flow" between indoors and outdoors.[11]

Of course, in the strict or literal sense of the words, the spatial flow through the glass walls of Johnson's house is no more Wrightian than his axial symmetry of door placement is Palladian. Nevertheless, these are useful comparative exaggerations with which to call the observer's attention to the most diverse and paradoxical of spatial elements present in this unique dwelling.

The resultant statement of Johnson's Glass House is ambiguous and perhaps even tinged with a quality of mock seriousness or profound wit. It brings to mind the romantic and sentimental attitudes of the mid- and later-18th century: the construction of sham ruins and follies in picturesque, naturalistic garden settings. These 18th-century garden structures, architectural conceits of almost two hundred years ago, marked the passage from the late Baroque order to the historical revival movements which, in turn, prepared the way for the emergence of 20th-century architecture. They were simultaneously characteristic phenomena of the *ancien régime* on the eve of its extinction and the framework in which new concepts of form and style—harbingers of 19th-century classic and gothic revivalism—first saw the light of day. In a similar way it is conceivable that the perplexing spatial insinuations of Johnson's glass gazebo and its surrounding "house" of natural forms herald a new architectural mode, though its exact relevance to any but the most specialized of domestic programs is not immediately apparent. In any event, the exploitation of the exterior spatial ambient of architectural volume, glazed or otherwise, is a most consistent and personally distinctive concern of Johnson's. It began in the extremely Miesian Johnson House, Cambridge, 1942 (plates 1 and 2), and culminates, at least for the moment, in the unique "outdoor room" (plate 107) of the New Harmony, Indiana, Roofless Church of 1960.

Johnson's preoccupation with the creation of exterior, freemoving spaces is further developed in two urban works of the early 1950's: the Guest House for John D. Rockefeller III, New York, 1950 (plates 18–20), and the Sculpture Court for the Museum of Modern Art, New York, 1953 (plates 39–42).

28 The former is a slight, elegant construction sandwiched in between two larger buildings of indifferent architectural distinction. Perhaps its most noteworthy feature is the atrium-like court with reflecting pool (plate 19) which occupies much of the rear half of the site. Here, Johnson has deliberately sacrificed a considerable area of interior space in favor of the court. In doing so, he has created spatial expansiveness despite the severe limitations of the site, which differs so extremely from the rural setting of the Glass House. In addition to providing an outdoor room, this design opened up the otherwise thoroughly closed-in living spaces of the Guest House, providing them with an unexpected sense of airiness and flow.

The Sculpture Court has even further surprises for an alert observer. Largely forced to utilize walls designed by others,[12] Johnson concentrated on the subtle leveling and terracing of the pavement itself, and on the placement of the reflecting pools. In addition, he provided a characteristically neutral yet beautifully proportioned screen wall on the garden's 54th Street side, effectively relieving its potential monotony by areas in which the brick gives way to wood slats. In this fashion, the sense of interior seclusion is just perceptibly modified, and the interior and exterior ambiguities suggested by the entire composition are of the utmost delicacy.

Two Johnson designs of 1956, the Eric Boissonnas House, New Canaan (plates 58–62), and the William A. M. Burden project, Mt. Kisco, New York (plates 55–57), further enrich the lively and sensitive spatial concepts and continue to re-examine the possible kinds of relation between interior and exterior. The monumental Burden project proposed a vast canopy conceived in much the same spirit that motivated Mies in his early 1950's projects for a Chicago Convention Hall. Within this total, universal space, demarcated but not enclosed by a broadly spaced peristyle of thin columns, were three sealed and enclosed cubic elements whose height was but one half that of the canopy. These provided separate accommodations for the living and dining area, master bedroom, and guest suite. The contemporary Boissonnas House is less overwhelmingly single-minded in its over-all design, and simultaneously marks a surface intensification of the latent romantic propensities in Johnson's domestic work. As a pergola-like structure combining interior and exterior spaces, it represents a reappraisal of the Glass House concepts of seven years before. In the case of the Boissonnas House,

the brick-piered pergolas, providing an exterior echo of
the cellular interior spaces, offer an irresistible analogy to the
Potsdam villas of the 1820's and '30's by Karl Friedrich
Schinkel.

The Johnsonian manner of spatial organization deserves
continued comment in considering his other houses of the
1950's, for it is in this aspect of his architecture that the personal, non-Miesian side of his work is most pronounced.
Mies's style has evolved over the past half-century in a way
that has led to greater and greater spatial simplicity and
regularity, with the concomitant suppression of separate elements. On the other hand, Johnson's work begins at a point
near where Mies leaves off, and persistently reconsiders the
entire problem in terms of the relationships of various elements, particularly interior compartments and exterior areas.
During the decade 1950–59, these re-introduced "elements"
gradually became more and more pronounced as distinct, individual spaces. Furthermore, Johnson's evolution toward a
greater sense of compartmentation and enclosure proceeds
hand in hand with the emergence of a solid, abstract
monumentality in his buildings of the later 1950's. In this
evolution away from the universal space of the 1949 Glass
House toward a more traditional mode of expression, the
George Oneto House, Irvington, New York, 1951; the Richard
Hodgson House, New Canaan, 1951; the Robert Wiley House,
also New Canaan, 1953; the Richard Davis House, Wayzata,
Minnesota, 1954; and the Robert Leonhardt House, Lloyd
Harbor, Long Island, 1956, represent a clearly defined se-
quential development.

The spatial organization of the George Oneto House
(plates 21–24), with its centrally located living room separat-
ing the kitchen and dining area on one side from the bedrooms
on another, is, in effect, the perfecting and regularizing of a
residential scheme that Johnson first used in his early Farney
House, Sagaponack, Long Island (plates 3 and 4), constructed
in 1946. Although reminiscent of the contemporary houses of
Marcel Breuer, the incisive and disciplined clarity of organization in the Farney House is in marked opposition to Breuer's
rather picturesque tendencies at that time. With the 1951
Oneto House, however, Johnson arrived at an even more
incisive mode of personal expression. If there are Miesian
qualities in the elevation as well as in the plan, if there is the
ghost of a "Palladian" discipline in the house's pseudo-cross-

30  axial symmetry, or if there is a "Wrightian" kind of spatial flow between inside and out, these influences have been totally transformed—indeed, sublimated—beyond specific recognition into Johnson's personal style. Indeed, although that style is the outgrowth of his scholarship and connoisseurship, and hence reflects his long familiarity with the sources, familiarity has made it possible for him to develop beyond, rather than remain subservient to, his models.

The exterior elevation system of the Richard Hodgson House (plates 25–28) seems to bear a resemblance to that of the Oneto House of the same year, but, as is so often the case with Johnson, the exterior shell is little more than the servant of the spaces contained by it. The first portion of the Hodgson House was built on a U-shaped plan around a glazed court, and the plan reveals an axial symmetry which is, superficially, both Miesian and Pompeian. However, the interior space is dominated by a cross-axial (indeed, non-axial) flow that is made possible by the glass walls that open both inward, toward the court, and outward. These major features actually vitiate the sense of rigid orthogonal or right-angled spatial organization, which is visible only at the principal entry. The ultimate effect appears balanced between the all-encompassing, unrestricted progressions of interior and exterior spatial relationship inherent in the Glass House and the more completely compartmented effects of his later work.

The 1953 Robert Wiley House (plates 34–37) represents a somewhat different departure. Tinged with eclecticism, its formal source is dual: Miesian for the glass cube, Corbusian for the rough masonry stylobate (specifically the de Mandrot House, Le Pradet, 1932, which in a more literal fashion influenced Johnson's early Booth House project of 1946). If the two elements are not of his own invention, their usage most certainly is. Two rival forms, one opaque and the other transparent, are unceremoniously, yet effectively, brought together so that the glass cube hovers lightly on top of its rugged base. The abrupt contrast of a solid with a crystalline form here is a restatement of the theme found in conjunction with the Glass House, where the Guest House was a materially inverted image of its transparent colleague. With this building, Johnson for the first time elevates the principal living area above ground level. In doing so, he evokes the precedents of Mies's Farnsworth House and Le Corbusier's earlier Villa Savoye (compare plates 14, 37 and 38). But it is the

concept, rather than particular formal and structural devices,
that is borrowed.

The two-story elevation of the Wiley House is an exception in Johnson's domestic design, and in the Richard Davis House of 1954 (plates 43–47) the elevated silhouette is replaced by an almost rambling layout of horizontal brick slab walls, interrupted at strategic points by areas of glass curtain wall. Largely because of the special requirements for this house, which demanded large areas of wall surface for the installation of a distinguished painting collection, this is the most inwardly oriented of Johnson's domestic projects. Indeed, the Davis House is, in effect, a private gallery, with a central light court completely glazed and isolated from the more literally "interior" spaces. In its organizational principle it anticipates the central space of the 1958–60 Munson-Williams-Proctor Institute. As in the 1951 Hodgson House the symmetrical plan with axis and cross-axis picked out by the four sliding panels of the central light court (echoing the usage of the Glass House itself) is not borne out in the perception of the total space whose unity is interrupted by the volume of the fireplace or the screen wall adjacent to one corner of the inner court. At the same time the unified quality of this space is never totally submerged by these various intrusions. The easy, relaxed way in which the over-all form is placed upon a terrace, encompassed by a similarly detailed brick wall, helps to reinforce and repeat on the exterior the smooth, fluent crosscurrents of space that occur on the interior. Furthermore, in its suggestion of lateral spatial movement through the adjustment of slablike elements, the Davis House is the one work by Johnson that is at all suggestive of Mies's early Barcelona Pavilion of 1929. Mies's Pavilion, of course, was likewise placed upon a podium which reinforced its irregular horizontality, and its exterior walls and interior partitions were similarly situated, slablike elements which set the otherwise static spaces in fluent, graceful motion. In its greater sense of a closed volume, in its more emphatic inward orientation, the Davis House materially differs in spatial principle from the Barcelona Pavilion.

Following the design of the Davis House by two years, the Robert Leonhardt House of 1956 (plates 50–54), with its boldly projecting glass-walled living area, is related to another Miesian paradigm. In this case Johnson followed his prototype, a 1934 sketch for a glass house on a hillside,[13] with

32    rather more precision than usual. The result is that the Leonhardt House is much more of a literal Miesian design than the Glass House itself, which, as has already been noted, deviates in significant matters of form and space from its prototype, the Farnsworth House. In other respects, the Leonhardt House is typical of the other domestic works of Johnson's first maturity. The landward wings are almost exclusively enclosed by brick curtain walls, thus providing the familiar abrupt and absolute contrast with the crystalline block projecting toward the water below.

None of these designs created during the five-year period 1951–56 provided much basis for anticipation of the turn in Johnson's development which was marked by the Eric Boissonnas House of 1956 (plates 58–62). The similarities between the Boissonnas House and the Romantic villas of Schinkel have already been noted. However superficial they may be, these resemblances to a relatively subjective Romantic style serve to remind us that Johnson, like every architect active in the mid-20th century, has in one fashion or another come under the shadow of an even more expressively romantic architect, Frank Lloyd Wright. From time to time Johnson has made studies that were rather literally in the manner of the great Midwestern architect, though none of these were ever brought to a finished state, let alone built. Nonetheless, certain particular kinds of spatial relationships which he has employed are long-term, indirect outgrowths of ideas that were first formulated by Wright more than a half-century ago. Curiously, there is the most general sort of similarity between the 1956 Boissonnas House and Wright's 1908 Evans House, Chicago, in that the central block stands up a full two stories, and is flanked on both sides by lower, veranda-like spurs.

While the Boissonnas House in no way captures the sense and idea of Wright's Prairie Style idiom (features such as the broadly projecting low-pitched hipped roofs being totally foreign to Johnson's design), this fortuitous and superficial resemblance affords the interested observer an excellent opportunity to reflect upon the parallels that exist between two of the most characteristically modern domestic architectural styles of the 20th century. Both Johnson and Wright were concerned with the expression and characterization of spatial relationships in a personal, original fashion. If each arrived finally and inevitably at a very different, unique solution, it does not invalidate the fact that, despite their individual and almost incompatible ways, both have worked with space as a

raw material in the invention of distinctively 20th-century     33
architectonic compositions. Traditionalist that he is, by this
one quality Johnson is nonetheless securely identified as an
architect of his own age and time. Whereas Wright, in the
Prairie houses, was seeking a subtly articulated, flowing con-
tinuum of space moving from large to small units, from out-
side to inside, by means of a gradual crescendo or diminuendo,
Johnson establishes his equally fascinating relationships by
seeking an identity in separated or articulated units. In this
respect, the interior and exterior spaces of the 1956 Boissonnas House represent a major and significant step forward
from the total, all-inclusive spatial configurations of the 1949
Glass House. The doubled size of the Boissonnas living area
(plate 60) is a monumental restatement of the standard
module employed throughout the interior. Its relationship to
the immediate outdoor surroundings is brought about not, in
the Wrightian fashion, by gesturing projections of wall plane
or low-hipped roof. Instead, the relationship is achieved
through the repetition of elements in both exterior and interior
design. Thus, the space of the living room (functionally a
glazed porch or pavilion) is repeated on the adjacent terrace
(functionally an outdoor living area); and, similarly, the
uniform brick piers of the pergola, which match the structural
piers of the house, are used as an element of exterior design
in conjunction with the walls themselves. As such, this intricate series of residential spaces would seem to represent
an extensive summation of Johnson's long-term preoccupation
with many facets of modern architecture: Schinkelesque,
Wrightian, and Miesian. The synthetic result is not eclectic in
the normal and casual sense of the word, however, for Johnson has brought invention as well as refinement to the spatial
problems. In his magnificent, intellectually grounded spatial
duplication (not interpenetration!) of interior and exterior
in the Boissonnas House, Johnson has brought the first phase
of his work to a vigorous conclusion. At the same time, he has
provided—at least in part—a point of departure for his
present, more overtly monumental phase. It is fitting, therefore, that the Boissonnas House is regarded by Johnson himself as representative of his best effort.

Since 1956, Johnson's energies have been increasingly de-
voted to large-scale non-domestic projects, whereas, until that
date, his creative development had been primarily in the field

of domestic work. It therefore seems reasonable to deduce that the monumentality latent in the 1956 Boissonnas House is at least in part the somewhat fortuitous consequence of his new involvement in the design of larger and more complex building types. This does not, however, preclude the influence of new compositional and creative urges.

As early as 1952, he had provided a handsomely proportioned design of a small office building for the Schlumberger Corporation in Ridgefield, Conn. (plates 29–32). This design showed but little change from the stylistic vocabulary of the Hodgson House of the previous year. In fact, some of the corridors and related spaces are quite intimately conceived, and anticipate effects analogous to the spacious gallery-like Davis House of 1954. Given its commercial function, the most conspicuous characteristic of the sophisticated Schlumberger design is its suburban domestic scale. Even the largely centralized, but not rigorously compartmentalized, plan follows the general principles found in his houses at this time.

With reference to both actual size and expression of monumental scale, Johnson's first significant step in the creation of large communal or public spaces was taken with the Synagogue for the Congregation Kneses Tifereth Israel in Port Chester, New York (plates 63–66). Although consistent with the austere geometric shapes and plain surfaces of his early work, the large rectilinear volume here assumes a more supple, familiarly substantial appearance. Gone is the glass wall, and with it the thin, fragile-seeming brick slab which was the inevitable masonry complement to the impalpable, massless glazed screen.[14] A sense of sturdy plasticity is further heightened by the addition of a domed oval vestibule as a contrast in front of the large façade. With white, precast concrete panels framing narrow slit windows of the façade, the whole rectilinear form is framed by the crisply expressed black steel frame. The dazzling, pure white effect of the exterior is carried through to the interior, which is brilliantly illuminated from concealed skylights above the suspended butterfly ceiling canopy. At the same time, a subdued colorism is introduced by the passage of some light through the colored glass of the side walls. A pleasing luminous balance is thus achieved, one which succeeds in providing a relief from the aggressive purism of the architecture itself, without, however, transforming it into a mystical world similar to that of dark, rich-hued Gothic interiors.

Nevertheless, one senses a reorientation in the traditionalist
aspect of Johnson's style. With the Boissonnas House, Mies
as an intermediary source is left behind in favor of tendencies that are directly derived from Romantic architecture.
Similarly, while Johnson's variant of the Miesian structural
cage in black steel is apparent throughout both the interior
and exterior of the Synagogue, the rippling undulations of its
shallowly curved butterfly vault provide a new, rhythmic
inflection for the interior space. It is possible to speculate that
Johnson has become influenced by late Roman Imperial
architecture, especially by its fondness for rounded, irregular,
undulating forms both in plan and in vaulting surface.[15]
Useful as this observation is, it would seem that a more
plausible and recent source for this type of spatial play, in
conjunction with largely concealed celestial lighting, is to be
found in the Romantic-Classic work of Sir John Soane,
Schinkel's English contemporary, whose habitual use of
domes, freely interpreted groin vaults, and mysterious sources
of illumination provides ample source for this aspect of the
enriched Johnsonian idiom.

Thus, 1956 seems to be a crucial year for Johnson, one in
which he decided to modify and temper the originally severe
and restrictive style that was outwardly derived from the new
American work of Mies van der Rohe. These new departures
in the work of Johnson, which led ultimately to more willfully
shaped and contoured work such as the successive projects for
the New York State Theater at Lincoln Center, New York,
1959–61, or the Rehovot, Israel, Nuclear Reactor should not
be regarded as a sudden stylistic metamorphosis and a simultaneous rejection of the simple, aristocratic aloofness of his
first mature phase.

The gradual way in which Johnson's style evolves into an
openly historicizing idiom is revealed in the master plan for
the University of St. Thomas, Houston, Texas (plate 70),
and in the auditorium and classroom buildings (plates 68, 69)
constructed there (forming the only portion of the complex
carried out so far). One is instantly struck with the brittle,
seemingly under-scaled steel columns of the balconies and
ground-level passages, which represent an extraordinarily re-
fined variant of the rational, static forms of Mies. However, a
comparison with Mies's master plan for the Illinois Institute
of Technology, together with some representative buildings on
that Chicago campus, reveals that certain almost-concealed

36   differences are perhaps more important than the similarities of external structural and decorative vocabulary. In commenting upon Mies's IIT master plan, Johnson has noted that the subtle order of the design could profitably be compared with a traditional, classically designed collegiate campus such as that by Thomas Jefferson for the University of Virginia, 1819–26. "Unlike the Jefferson campus, order is not dependent on axial groupings" in the Mies scheme.[16] In effect, the geometrical autonomy of Mies's articulated rectilinear building cubes has almost no hierarchical or centrifugal relationship with a larger whole. A similar static tension between neighboring geometrical forms (one of Mies's most unique inventions) is employed by Johnson in the relationship between his Glass House and its subsidiary Guest House.

In the general scheme for the various elements in the University of St. Thomas master plan of 1957, Johnson has organized buildings of somewhat picturesque irregularity around a central mall, creating an effect spiritually close to the precedent of Jefferson's University. Simultaneously, he has provided sheltered walkways and covered passages which surround and link the various separate elements, and these, too, recall the design for the University of Virginia. The result is a thoroughly un-Miesian unity and interrelationship of parts, in spite of the glass, metal, and brick elevations. The University of St. Thomas is thus a blend of Mies's Industrial Classicism of the 1940's with the Romantic Classicism of the 1820's, and once more Johnson demonstrates the depth of his historical perception (compare plates 70, 71A and 71B).

Romantic and Industrial Classicism is also the fitting label for the museum gallery building of the Munson-Williams-Proctor Institute, Utica, New York, 1957–60 (plates 72, 74, 76–83). Widely heralded as Johnson's last "Miesian" design, it is in fact only superficially in accord with the manner of the elder architect. A somber, granite-faced cube of imposing size, suspended between an equally monumental concrete frame revetted in bronze, this powerful monumental form is sited on a gently sloping terrain so that the street façade, situated on the higher ground, is in effect placed in a dry moat. This ditch partially obscures the fact that the basement is enclosed only by a glass wall—a device that ensures the appreciation of the fact that the basic geometric block is suspended within the giant concrete-and-bronze frame. The result is a curiously mannerist kind of inversion, Johnson's modern palazzo being fitted out not with the expected rusticated basement, but with its exact and seemingly inappropriate opposite.

It might well be asked why a contemporary monument should be evaluated by reference to 15th- and 16th-century Renaissance criteria. Underneath the outward cloak of modernism (the superficial Miesian element) Johnson has provided a design that is fundamentally traditional and classicizing; a design that stresses dramatically enclosed spatial compartments. In contrast, Mies's designs for museums, especially his project for a Museum for a Small City of 1942,[17] are radically different, composed of freely situated elements placed within an over-all universal space. Invariably there is an implicit sense of lateral movement which makes these spaces akin to those of the Barcelona Pavilion of 1929. While there is a noticeable influence of this Miesian museum scheme in the layout of the Davis House, 1954, this freedom is largely foreign to the more frankly academic organizational principles utilized by Johnson in his design for the Proctor Institute. Comparison of the Proctor Institute building with Mies's contemporary Cullinan Wing of the Houston Museum of Fine Arts, 1958–59 (compare plates 72 and 73), illustrates other notable differences between the two architects. This is true despite a superficial rapport in the simplified, austere detailing of both structures and despite the fact that both structures are achieved with the use of large exterior girders. The entry to Johnson's gallery is through a low, confining portal that effectively separates interior from exterior, whereas Mies's entry is through a glazed wall that occupies the full height of the three central bays in this gently curved façade. In Mies's design there is a reciprocal continuation of interior to exterior and, conversely, of exterior to interior space, in contrast to the separateness which is so inescapable in the Proctor Institute.

Consequently, Johnson's museum is a notable landmark in the development of American architecture in the late 1950's, reflecting a deep-rooted urge to re-establish sensible contact with those elements of the pre-modern architectural tradition—the very elements which had been rejected by the first two generations of 20th-century architects as a consequence of new concepts of space and form. The interior spaces of the Proctor Institute, and especially the monumental two-story central room, with its elegantly detailed balustrades

**38** on the stair and gallery, puzzle the visitor who seeks to understand the building in terms of radical 20th-century spatial aesthetics. It is infinitely more appropriate to subject this space to a comparison with the stair wells of Germanic Romantic Classicism[18] than to analyze it in association with 20th-century principles pertaining to formal dislocations and ambiguities of a cubistic sort. Another analogy can be found in Le Corbusier's Tokyo Museum, 1957–59, itself a closed structure containing a large central space. However, Le Corbusier here achieved regularity without recourse to academic symmetry, and his expression of monumentality is spontaneous in contrast to Johnson's calculated reserve. Furthermore, Le Corbusier's structure is not paradoxically suspended but, instead, expressively supported by *piloti* underneath.

The retrospective, historicizing quality of Johnson's Proctor Institute is certainly the result of careful deliberation. It probably represents the first masterpiece of a recent architectural movement which seeks to discover for itself new sources of stimuli in the almost pretentiously conservative academic techniques. Under these circumstances, a further comparison of Johnson's neo-traditional museum with Wright's idiosyncratic Guggenheim Museum is provocative (compare plates 75 and 78). Designed as early as 1943, the Guggenheim was not built until the late 1950's, a time when the Proctor Institute building was under construction. Wright's concept—an unfolding, continuous, almost endless gallery space, realized through the use of the spiral ramp—would seem totally unrelated either stylistically or psychically to the static, finite space at the center of the Johnson gallery. Nevertheless, both designs are distinctively 20th-century metamorphoses of the Baroque and post-Baroque stair well as applied to the specific function of an exhibition space. Superficially, each realizes its goals through the application of an up-to-date, contemporary style. Yet each is implicitly negative and anti-modern in some if not all of its basic features. In addition to incorporating the similar device of a central exhibition space (even though they are conceived as entirely different shapes), both structures have a theater or auditorium situated in the basement directly under the area of major interest. In the Guggenheim Museum, Wright would seem to have invented a space of personal inflection and meaning. Yet its round form emphasized by the overhead dome (regrettably detailed in its final execution), its over-all simplicity of surface, and its ingenious effort to provide indirect lighting for the gallery walls would seem to lead back to equivalent Romantic-Classic effects found in the work of Soane and Schinkel. Similar influences are evidenced in Johnson's Port Chester Synagogue of 1956. While Wright's forms do not often have a literal derivation from works of the past, an implicit suggestion of subconscious prototypes is present in his works. Not surprisingly, Johnson's techniques and procedures in this area seem to be deliberate choices of derivation and inspiration—whereas Wright's are not always rationally demonstrable as specific stimuli.

In spite of these surface inconsistencies, however, the museums of both Johnson and Wright contribute to the development of a historically based attitude that is one of the most characteristic features of architecture in the early 1960's. At the same time, it must be understood that the historical point which may be the basis for this current tradition lies not very far behind the threshold of radical 20th-century architecture. In a sense the present reaction is perhaps no more than an effort at consolidation and introspective examination prior to a new and even more radical stylistic departure. In any event, the most recent of Johnson's completed works, together with various projects under construction, would seem to point in this direction. Most of these new works develop some theme that has been stated before in his designs, but with a new emphasis upon expressive monumentality, or habitual and traditional space configurations. The Amon Carter Museum of Western Art, Fort Worth, Texas (plates 84–88), finished in 1961, offers in its plan, interior spacing, exterior peristylar screen, and mammoth terrace leading from its façade, one of the most carefully thought-out instances of the new architectural conservatism. Perhaps the least consequential quality about this new formalism—as it has frequently been called— is the forms themselves. Here in the Carter Museum the sleek, carefully considered contours of reverse-tapered columns and flat segmental arches are quite striking, and yet their forms make little or no specific contribution to the characterization of either the interior or exterior spaces for which they act as normal boundary stones. The plan (plate 88) gives some inkling of the astute interrelationship between interior and exterior, as well as of the way in which the colossal exterior terrace and stylobate reduce the volume of the building to something remarkably diminutive. The interior of the Carter

40    Museum is formed by a U-shaped wall. This wall also marks
the ultimate termination of the exterior space, which begins
on a lower level at the far end of the terrace, and proceeds up
a series of low embankments and retaining walls, passing at a
mid-point a major cross axis which provides the principal
entry to the sequence of open and closed spaces.

The relation of the Amon Carter and the Proctor museum
buildings to the project for the Sheldon Art Gallery (plates
90, 91), for the University of Nebraska at Lincoln, (currently
under construction), is still difficult to assess, given the se-
verely limited material available for current study of the
building. However, the view of the façade as revealed in the
model suggests the continued exploration of tapered and curving pier forms which have appeared in Johnson's recent designs. The interior spaces (whose stair hall can be glimpsed
through the recessed entry vestibule) probably will not be
developed along the lines of the relative suppleness and
plasticity of the exterior shapes. Indeed, a contrast of the
balanced, symmetrical entry spaces of the Sheldon Art
Gallery project with the more open and apparently spontaneous vestibule and stair well of Le Corbusier's High Court at
Chandigarh is interesting. Such a comparison indicates that
Johnson's current development in the creation of spaces is
not toward the use of increasingly fluid sequences, but rather
toward the employment of more enclosed, contrasted spaces
with clearly disciplined, compartmentalized elements. Thus,
the Sheldon Art Gallery project would appear to have a more
direct relationship with Schinkel's Altes Museum than with
the contemporary High Court at Chandigarh (compare plates
89A, 89B and 90).

Similar problems surround the various projects for the
unfinished New York State Theater at Lincoln Center
(plates 92–97). The circular elevation of the first project is
dominated by a monumental concrete frame on the exterior.
In a subsequent study for the mass of the theater itself, this
exterior structure is rejected in favor of more aggressive
modeling and shaping; but the present definitive project re-
jects this expressionist idiom in favor of a façade more soberly
and rationally academic in principle, more incisively articulated with respect to establishing a relationship between the
paired vertical piers and the horizontal elements. It is not
possible to venture further than this on the basis of current

information; but this New York State Theater promises to be
one of Johnson's major works of the 1960's.

Although Johnson also prepared three alternate façades for the Asia House, New York (plates 100–102), finished in 1960, these designs are by no means an exact mirror of the considerable changes that have transpired in the successive projects for the Lincoln Square Theater. Something of the chameleon-like character of recent architectural design in general can be appreciated by studying the very restricted range of possibilities for the Asia House façade, and by the realization that each of the three alternatives was of an inherently individual and unique character. The version executed in 1960 is an aristocratic black and silver study in large and small panels with a tendency toward faint decorative mannerism. In comparison, the somewhat similar glass façade for Johnson's earlier Museum of Modern Art Annex (plate 67) is simpler and more straight-forward in the general proportions of the glass panels and is deliberately constructed in a more markedly Miesian manner of expression.

A more complete idea of Johnson's present growth and evolution can be obtained by a study of two recently completed and rather unorthodox buildings, which may in some respects offer token gestures in the direction of evolving new architectonic concepts, patterns, and relationships. The first of these is the so-called Roofless Church, or Shrine, at New Harmony, Indiana, finished in 1960 (plates 104–107); the second is the similarly plotted but differently shaped Nuclear Reactor at Rehovot, Israel, finished in 1961 (plates 108–112). The New Harmony Shrine is in one major respect another vast outdoor room, and thereby develops an idea first stated by Johnson in the Glass House of 1949, and later in the sweeping terraces of the Amon Carter Museum, Fort Worth. The space is formed by a thin high wall surrounding a regular and nearly symmetrically disposed temenos. A major axis is formed by the entry in the short side and the shingled ciborium in the form of a high lobed dome which shelters a diminutive Lipchitz sculpture. A slightly irregular cross-axis, which does not intersect the principal one at a right angle, is formed by an entrance set off-center in one long side and by a projecting loggia that looks out from the quasi-interior space. It is this unroofed space which gives the whole complex its most distinctive quality. The intricate relationships between the various spaces and focal points imply that this "interior" should

42  not be thought of simply as a paved garden any more than should the Sculpture Court at the Museum of Modern Art.

Like the New Harmony Roofless Church, the Nuclear Reactor is composed of a low horizontal mass above which rises a distinctively shaped architectural form. There ends the similarity. Unlike the delicacy of the contrasting shingle and brick forms of the unusual New Harmony edifice, the Rehovot Reactor is a massive, rugged form molded in concrete. The battered slope of the outer perimeter walls is suggestively "Mesopotamian," and at the same time is more directly associated with a non-Miesian, non-Romantic-Classic element in recent architecture, which puts a premium upon the invention of appropriate yet subjective and emotion-stimulating exterior shapes. The solid, closed, protective character of this building is somewhat mitigated by the glazed courtyard, with its projecting slab supported by vigorously profiled reverse-taper piers that add a further sense of rugged plasticity to this striking building. What exactly its role will be in the light of Johnson's subsequent designs of the middle and late 1960's is of course impossible to predict. Nonetheless, its creative potential must be recognized as a rare instance of subjective invention on the part of an architect who has usually been content to leave the creation of robust new shapes to others. In this building Johnson comes close, not to emulation of the recent forms of Wright, Le Corbusier, or even Saarinen, but rather to an equivalently creative verve.

Two further projects by Johnson were completed during the same years, 1960–61. The first is a unit of dormitories at Sarah Lawrence College, Bronxville, New York (plate 115), whose design and structure are framed by a rank of concrete columns supporting low segmental arches that also form the building's cornice. The remainder of the three-story structure is clad in brick. The square casement windows add an unexpected touch to the generously proportioned fenestration system, and the sloping site is used to advantage in articulating the three elements of the dormitory with respect to one another. The second completed building is the Computing Laboratory, Brown University, Providence, Rhode Island, of 1961 (plate 113). Here, on a reduced scale, is a variant of the concrete framework with cross-pieces forming a cornice, that first appeared in the early, discarded project for the Lincoln Center Theater. In contrast to the highly inventive forms of the Roofless Church at New Harmony and the Rehovot Reactor,

neither of these two buildings seems as important a step in $\quad$ 43
the development of Johnson's continuing style. Rather, their
subsequent importance will probably lie in their transitional,
somewhat uncommitted character.

Taken as a group, the most recent Johnson works—those of
the last five or six years—are undeniably less homogeneous
in appearance than those of the preceding decade. It is, therefore, more difficult to arrive at generalizations that will fit the
entire group. This condition is in contrast to the deliberate
sequential growth that was so conspicuous in the work of the
early and middle 1950's. Thus, Johnson's buildings of
the present indicate three distinct, and sometimes opposing,
facets of architectural reality: an ebb tide in the development
of a new architecture, as in the case of the Sarah Lawrence
Dormitories; a venturing into a new realm of creative activity,
as in the Rehovot Reactor; and a determined effort to regain
certain stylistic conceptions of the classic and academic past
while retaining a nominally modern vernacular style, as in
the Utica Museum. Each of these simultaneous facets represents an essential part of Philip Johnson's current architectural endeavor. To say at this juncture which will, in the
long run, prove the most durable and significant would be
impertinent, intemperate, and unwise.

# Notes to the Text

1. This term first obtained currency in Henry-Russell Hitchcock and Philip Johnson, *The International Style: Architecture since 1922*, New York, 1932. More recently, Hitchcock has maintained that the term was proposed to the authors by Alfred H. Barr. See Henry-Russell Hitchcock, *Architecture, Nineteenth and Twentieth Centuries*, Baltimore, 1958, pp. 380, 454, note 1.

2. Philip Johnson, *Mies van der Rohe*, New York, 1947; second edition, 1953.

3. While the design of the Seagram Building has been invariably attributed both to Mies van der Rohe and to Philip Johnson, the latter disclaims credit for the design, and it has thus seemed appropriate that it not be illustrated in this book. On the other hand, the interiors of the Four Seasons Restaurant in the Seagram Building are illustrated (plates 98, 99), as they are Johnson's own personal creation.

4. After completing this manuscript I discovered the following interesting characterization of Johnson by Vincent Scully, "Johnson at his best is admirably lucid, unsentimental, and abstract, with the most ruthlessly aristocratic, highly studied taste of anyone practicing in America today. All that nervous sensibility, lively intelligence, and a stored mind can do, he does. One must take him as he is." From Vincent Scully, Jr., *Modern Architecture, The Architecture of Democracy*, New York, 1961, p. 118, note 41.

5. Robert Motherwell, quoted by Sam Hunter in the chapter, "U.S.A.," in *Art Since 1945*, New York, Abrams, 1958, p. 288.

6. For one interpretation of Wright's late works, see Vincent Scully, Jr., *Frank Lloyd Wright*, New York, 1960, pp. 28–32.

7. Johnson's publication of the Glass House in *The Architectural Review*, CVIII, No. 645, September 1950, pp. 152–59, with its specific citation of numerous prototypes and suggestions which influenced his own design, is surely a landmark not just in the history of architectural journalism (one which is not even approximated in the heyday of nineteenth-century eclecticism), but in the development of contemporary architectural theory as well.

8. *Idem*.

9. Philip Johnson, *Mies van der Rohe*, p. 162.

10. It is important to note that Mies's court-house type is an "earth-hugging" variant of the air-borne Le Corbusier house on stilts, the Villa Savoye, Poissy, 1929–31. The terrace of the Le Corbusier *piano nobile*, and its relationship to the adjacent glass-walled living space, is quite similar to Mies's design. This is indicative of the complex relationships and exchanges of ideas that went on among the older practitioners of the modern manner some thirty years ago.

11. Henry-Russell Hitchcock, "The Current Work of Philip Johnson," *Zodiac*, VIII, 1961, p. 66.

12. Philip L. Goodwin and Edward O. Stone designed the garden façade of the Museum proper; and a variety of architects, including Wallace Harrison for the 1936 brick flats directly across the street and Charles F. McKim for the University Club further east at the corner of Fifth Avenue, are responsible for works gracing the northern side of West 54th Street.

13. Johnson, *Mies van der Rohe*, p. 109.

14. The transformation of Johnson's style, and its evolution away from that of Mies can be appreciated when the Port Chester Synagogue is compared with the older architect's 1952 Chapel at the Illinois Institute of Technology. In Mies's rigorous design the nature of the static spatial problem, the self-effacing details, and the tacit relationship between interior and exterior space that is brought about by the glass-wall façade, result in a solution that might be called "Technological Classicism." Conversely, Johnson's Synagogue is a closed, visually isolated volume which is entered through the preparatory space of a vestibule. Hence, it is more conventional, even Romantic or Academic in its "Classicism," although its Miesian heritage remains reasonably conspicuous in many of its details.

15. Vincent Scully, Jr., *Modern Architecture*, p. 35.

16. Johnson, *Mies van der Rohe*, p. 137.

17. *Ibid.*, pp. 174–79.

18. The most relevant comparison would seem to be the entry spaces of Schinkel's Altes Museum, Berlin, 1824–28, with its stairs recessed behind the long peristyle of the principal façade (see plate 89B).

| | |
|---|---|
| 1906 | Born July 8 in Cleveland, Ohio |
| 1923–30 | Harvard University, A.B., class of 1927 |
| 1930–36 | Department of Architecture, Museum of Modern Art, New York |
| 1932 | Published *The International Style: Architecture Since 1922* in collaboration with Henry-Russell Hitchcock |
| 1942 | Johnson House, Ash Street, Cambridge, Mass. (plates 1, 2) |
| 1943 | B. Arch., Graduate School of Design, Harvard University |
| 1946 | Farney House, Sagaponack, Long Island, N.Y. (plates 3, 4) |
| 1946–54 | Director, Department of Architecture and Design, Museum of Modern Art, New York |
| 1947 | Published first edition of *Mies van der Rohe*, Museum of Modern Art, New York |
| 1949 | Glass House, his own residence, New Canaan, Conn., completed after three years of design (plates 5–13, 15–16) |
| 1950 | Museum of Modern Art Annex (plate 67) |
| | Rockefeller Guest House, New York (plates 18–20) |
| 1951 | Hodgson House, New Canaan, Conn. (25–28) |
| | Oneto House, Irvington, N.Y. (plates 21–24) |
| 1952 | Schlumberger Administration Building, Ridgefield, Conn. (plates 29–32) |
| 1953 | Second edition of *Mies van der Rohe* |
| | Ball House, New Canaan, Conn. (plate 33) |
| | Sculpture Court, Museum of Modern Art, New York (plates 39–42) |
| | Wiley House, New Canaan, Conn. (plates 34–37) |
| | House for Wiley Development Company, New Canaan, Conn. (plates 48, 49) |
| 1954 | Davis House, Wayzata, Minnesota (plates 43–47) |
| 1956 | Leonhardt House, Lloyd Harbor, Long Island, N.Y. (plates 50–54) |
| | Boissonnas House I, New Canaan, Conn. (plates 58–62) |
| | Synagogue for Congregation Kneses Tifereth Israel, Port Chester, N.Y. (plates 63–66) |
| 1957 | University of St. Thomas, Auditorium and Classroom Buildings, Houston, Texas (plates 68–70) |
| 1958 | Four Seasons Restaurant, New York (plates 98, 99) |
| 1960 | Asia House, New York City (plates 100–102) |
| | Museum Building for Munson-Williams-Proctor Institute, Utica, N.Y. (plates 72, 74, 76–83) |
| | Roofless Church, Robert Lee Blaffer Trust, New Harmony, Indiana (plates 104–107) |
| | Sarah Lawrence Dormitories, Bronxville, N.Y. (plate 115) |

1961    Amon Carter Museum of Western Art, Fort Worth, Texas    47
        (plates 84–88)
        Nuclear Reactor, Israel Atomic Energy Commission, Re-
        hovot, Israel (plates 108–112)
        Computing Laboratory, Brown University, Providence,
        R.I. (plate 113)

*Works Under Construction, Spring, 1962:*
        New York State Theater, Lincoln Center, New York City
        (plates 92–97)
        Sheldon Art Gallery, University of Nebraska, Lincoln,
        Neb. (plates 89, 91)
        St. Anselm's Abbey, Washington, D.C.
        Johnson Pavilion, New Canaan, Conn. (plate 103)
        Boissonnas House II, Cap Bénat, France (plate 116)
        Museum Wing, Dumbarton Oaks, Washington, D.C.

1.   *Johnson House, Ash Street, Cambridge, Massachusetts, 1942–43. Interior looking toward court. (Photo: Ezra Stoller)*

2.   *Johnson House. Plan.*

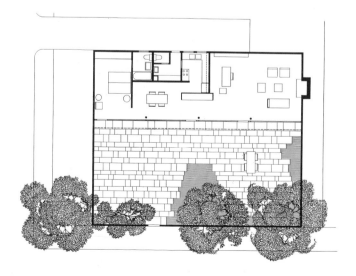

3. *Eugene Farney House, Sagaponack, Long Island, New York, 1946. Exterior. (Photo: Ezra Stoller)*

4. *Farney House. Plan.*

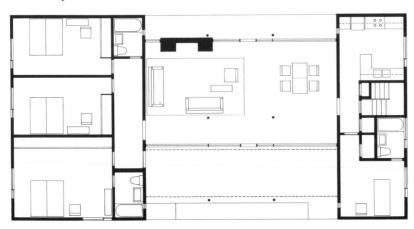

5.  *Philip Johnson Residence, New Canaan, Connecticut, 1949. Glass House. Entrance façade.*

6.  *Johnson Residence. Glass House at right.*
    *Guest House at left. (Photo: Ezra Stoller)*

7.  *Johnson Residence. Glass House at left.*
    *Guest House in background. (Photo: Ezra Stoller)*

8.  *Johnson Residence. Glass House. Night view of interior. (Photo: Ezra Stoller)*

9.  *Johnson Residence. Glass House. Night view.*

10.  *Johnson Residence. Glass House. Interior, living and dining area.*

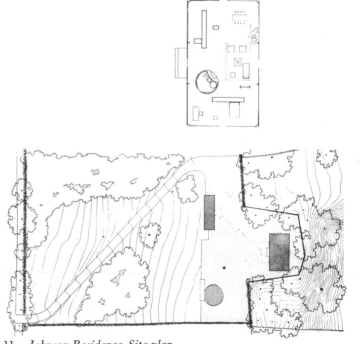

11.  *Johnson Residence. Site plan.*

12.   *Johnson Residence. Glass House. Living area.*

13.   *Johnson Residence. Glass House.
      View and reflection in wall.*

14. *Mies van der Rohe. Farnsworth House. Exterior.*
    *(Designed 1946, executed 1951.)*

15. *Johnson Residence. Glass House. Side façade.*

16.   *Johnson Residence. Guest House. Interior. (Photo: Ezra Stoller)*

17. *House Project for Kootz Gallery Exhibit, 1951. View of model (developed from an early scheme for the Glass House).*

18. *Rockefeller Guest House, New York, 1950. Street façade.*

19.   *Rockefeller Guest House. Interior from bedroom toward court.*

20.   *Rockefeller Guest House. Plan.*

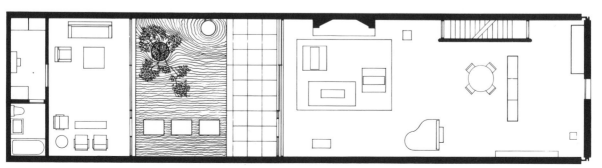

21. *George Oneto House, Irvington-on-Hudson, New York, 1951. Entrance façade. (Photo: Ezra Stoller)*

22. *Oneto House. Garden façade.*

23.  *Oneto House. Interior, living area. (Photo: Ezra Stoller)*

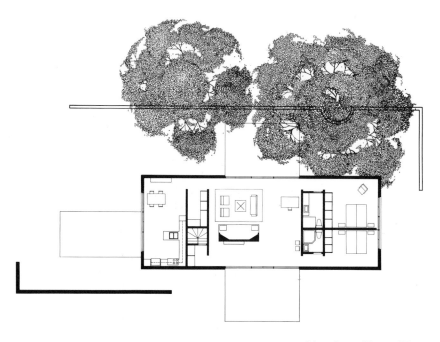

24.  *Oneto House. Plan.*

25.   *Richard Hodgson House, New Canaan, Connecticut, 1951. Entrance façade. (Photo: Ezra Stoller)*

26.   *Hodgson House. Rear façade. (Photo: Ezra Stoller)*

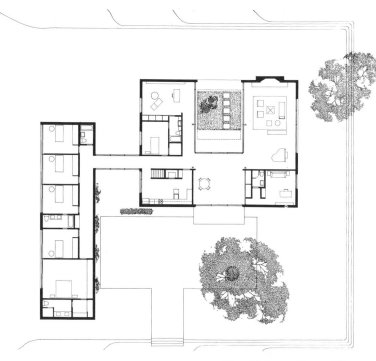

27. *Hodgson House. Plan.*

28. *Hodgson House. Interior, view across court toward living area. (Photo: Ezra Stoller)*

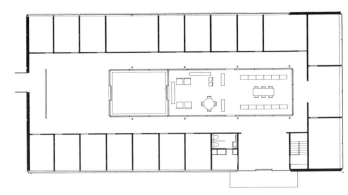

29. *Schlumberger Administration Building,*
*Ridgefield, Connecticut, 1952. Plan.*

30. *Schlumberger Administration Building. Entrance façade.*

31. *Schlumberger Administration Building. Rear façade.*

32.  *Schlumberger Administration Building. Interior looking toward court.*

33.  *Alice Ball House, New Canaan, Connecticut, 1953. (Photo: Ezra Stoller)*

34.  *Robert Wiley House, New Canaan, Connecticut, 1953.*
     *Exterior looking across terrace. (Photo: Ezra Stoller)*

35.  *Wiley House. Interior of living area. (Photo: Ezra Stoller)*

36. *Wiley House. Exterior. (Photo: Ezra Stoller)*

37.  *Wiley House. Exterior. (Photo: Ezra Stoller)*

38.  *Le Corbusier. Villa Savoye, Poissy, 1929–31. Exterior.*

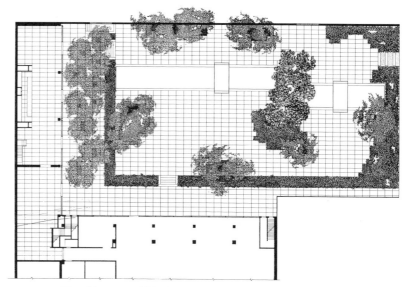

39.   *Museum of Modern Art, New York. Sculpture Court, 1953. Plan.*

40.   *Sculpture Court. View looking west. (The façade to the left is by Goodwin and Stone; the façade in the center is by Johnson.) (Photo: Ezra Stoller)*

41.  *Sculpture Court. View looking north.*

42.  *Sculpture Court. View looking east.*

43. *Richard Davis House, Wayzata, Minnesota, 1954.*
    *Exterior seen from terrace.*

44. *Davis House. Exterior seen from below terrace. (Photo: Ezra Stoller)*

45. *Davis House. Interior.*

46.   *Davis House. Interior. (Photo: Ezra Stoller)*

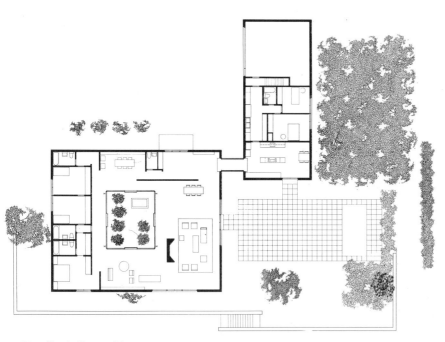

47.   *Davis House. Plan.*

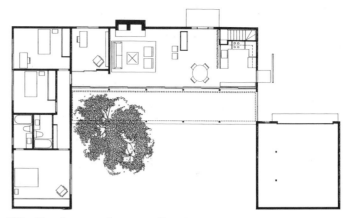

48. *House for Wiley Development Company, New Canaan, Connecticut, 1953. Plan.*

49. *House for Wiley Development Company. Exterior. (Photo: Ezra Stoller)*

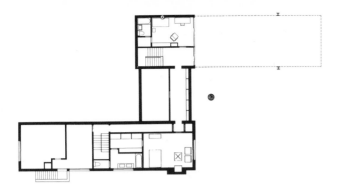

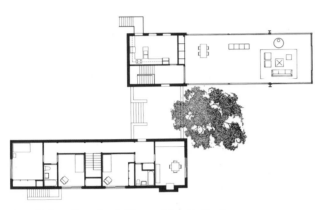

50. *Robert Leonhardt House, Lloyd's Neck,
    Long Island, New York, 1956. Plan.*

51. *Leonhardt House. Exterior, view of glass living area. (Photo: Ezra Stoller)*

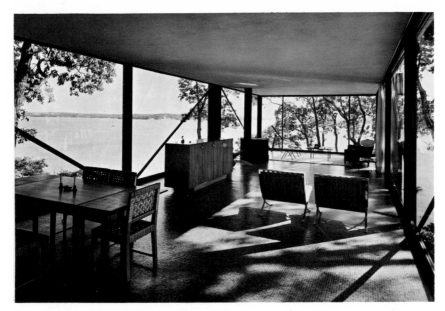

52.   *Leonhardt House. Interior of living area. (Photo: Ezra Stoller)*

53.   *Leonhardt House. Entrance terrace. (Photo: Ezra Stoller)*

55. *Project for William A. M. Burden House,*
    *Mt. Kisco, New York, 1956. Plan.*

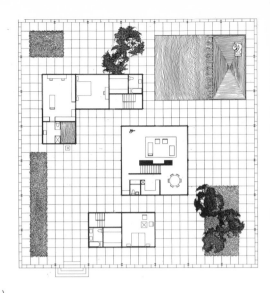

56. *Project for Burden House. View of model. (Photo: Ezra Stoller)*

57. *Project for Burden House. View of model. (Photo: Ezra Stoller)*

58.   *Eric Boissonnas House, New Canaan, Connecticut, 1956. Exterior seen from below terrace. (Photo: Ezra Stoller)*

59. *Boissonnas House. Exterior, living area. (Photo: Ezra Stoller)*

60. *Boissonnas House. Plan.*

61.   *Boissonnas House. Interior, living area. (Photo: Ezra Stoller*

62.   *Boissonnas House. Exterior looking toward entrance. (Photo: Ezra Stoller)*

63.   *Kneses Tifereth Israel Synagogue, Port Chester, New York, 1956. Entrance façade. (Photo: Ezra Stoller)*

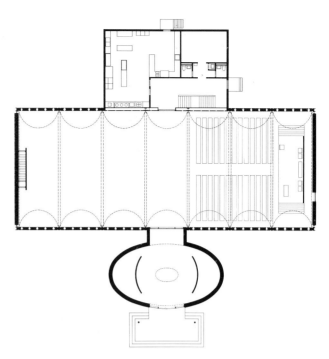

64. *Kneses Tifereth Israel Synagogue. Plan.*

65. *Kneses Tifereth Israel Synagogue. Interior. (Photo: Ezra Stoller)*

66. *Kneses Tifereth Israel Synagogue. Interior. (Photo: Ezra Stoller)*

67. *Museum of Modern Art Annex, New York, 1950. Façade facing 53rd Street. (Façade of main building at right by Goodwin and Stone, 1939.)*

68.   *University of St. Thomas, Houston, Texas. Auditorium and Classroom Buildings, 1957. View from the street.*

69.   *St. Thomas Auditorium and Classroom Buildings. View from the unfinished mall.*

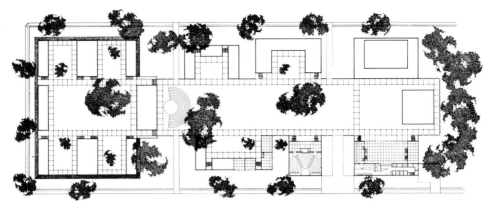

70. *University of St. Thomas. Master plan.*

71A. *Thomas Jefferson. University of Virginia. Master Plan. (From an engraving of 1856.)*

71B. *Mies van der Rohe. A group of three buildings at Illinois Institute of Technology, Chicago, Illinois, 1940–48.*

72.   *Munson-Williams-Proctor Institute, Utica, New York, 1957–60. Street Façade.*

73.   *Mies van der Rohe. Cullinan Wing, Museum of Fine
Arts, Houston, Texas, 1958–59. Façade.*

74.   *Munson-Williams-Proctor Institute. Entrance bridge over grass moat. (Photo: Ezra Stoller)*

75. *Frank Lloyd Wright. Guggenheim Museum,*
*New York, 1943–59. Interior.*

76. *Munson-Williams-Proctor Institute. Exterior, side view. (Photo: Ezra Stoller)*

77. *Munson-Williams-Proctor Institute. Site plan.*

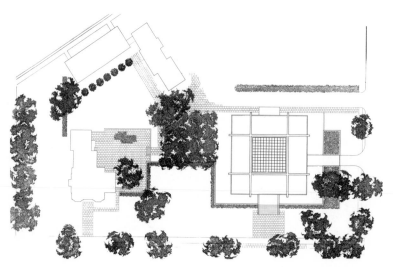

78.  *Munson-Williams-Proctor Institute. Interior, central space seen from gallery. (Photo: Ezra Stoller)*

79.  *Munson-Williams-Proctor Institute. Interior, central stairs from below. (Photo: Ezra Stoller)*

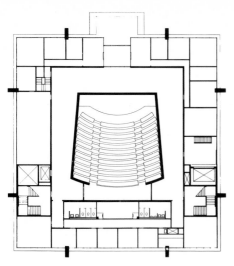

80.  *Munson-Williams-Proctor Institute. Ground-floor plan.*

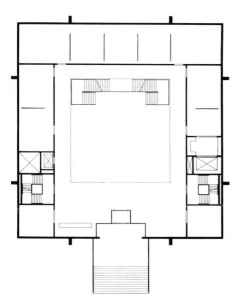

81.  *Munson-Williams-Proctor Institute. Main-floor plan.*

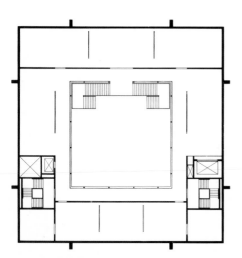

82.  *Munson-Williams-Proctor Institute. Balcony plan.*

83.  *Munson-Williams-Proctor Institute. Section.*

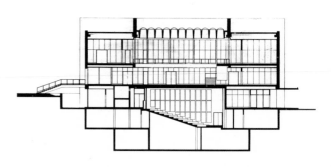

84.   *Amon Carter Museum of Western Art, Fort Worth, Texas, 1961. Exterior, principal façade. (Photo: Ezra Stoller)*

85.   *Amon Carter Museum. Interior of gallery.*
     *(Photo: Ezra Stoller)*

86.   *Amon Carter Museum. Exterior from below terrace. (Photo: Ezra Stoller)*

87. *Amon Carter Museum. Exterior, principal façade. (Photo: Ezra Stoller)*

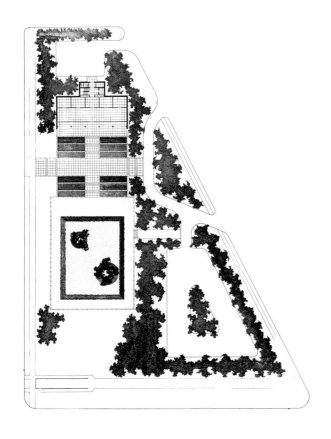

88. *Amon Carter Museum. Plan.*

89A.  *Le Corbusier. High Court Building, Chandigarh, 1951–56.*
*Detail of west façade.*

89B.  *K. F. Schinkel. Altes Museum, Berlin, 1824–28. Façade.*

90.  *Sheldon Art Gallery, University of Nebraska, Lincoln, Nebraska. Under construction 1962. Model.*

91.  *Sheldon Art Gallery. Travertine arches erected in Italy
to test the play of shadows.*

92.  *New York State Theater, Lincoln Center, New York City. Under construction 1962.
Model of authorized version. (Photo: Ezra Stoller)*

93. *Lincoln Center Plaza. Preliminary study (rejected), 1958.*

94. *Lincoln Center Plaza. Preliminary study (rejected), 1958. Entrance arcade.*

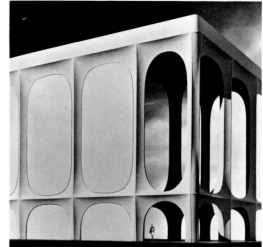

97. *New York State Theater. Second version. Detail of elevation.*

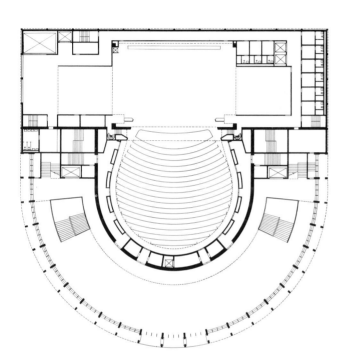

95. *New York State Theater. First version (rejected), 1958. Orchestra-floor plan.*

96. *New York State Theater. First version (rejected). Exterior.*

98.   *Four Seasons Restaurant, Seagram Building, New York, 1958. South room.*

99.   *Four Seasons Restaurant. North room.*

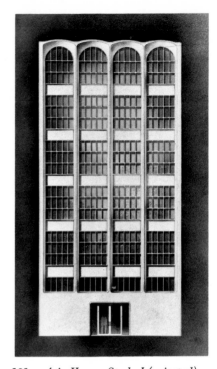

101. *Asia House. Study I (rejected).*

100. *Asia House, New York, 1960. Façade facing 64th Street.*

102.  *Asia House. Study II (rejected).*

103.  *Philip Johnson Pavilion, New Canaan, Connecticut. Under construction 1962. Model.*

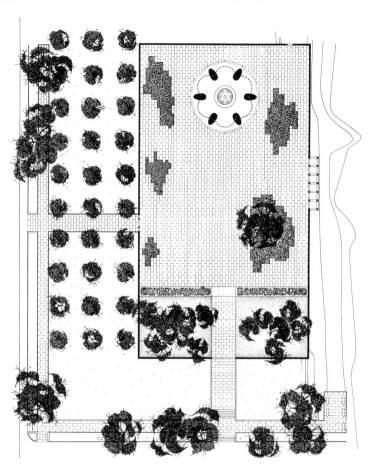

105. *Roofless Church. Plan.*

104. *Roofless Church for Robert Lee Blaffer Trust, New Harmony, Indiana, 1960. View of canopy.*

106. *Roofless Church. View from the south.*

107. *Roofless Church. Entrance.*

108.   *Nuclear Reactor, Rehovot, Israel, 1961. View into court.*

109. *Nuclear Reactor. Columns of the court.*

110. *Nuclear Reactor. View into court.*

111. *Nuclear Reactor. Exterior, general view.*

112. *Nuclear Reactor. Exterior, general view.*

113.  *Computing Laboratory, Brown University, Providence, Rhode Island, 1961. Exterior.*

114. *Kline Science Tower, Yale
University, New Haven,
Connecticut. Project, 1962.
(Construction scheduled for 1963.)*

115.  *Sarah Lawrence College Dormitories, Bronxville, New York, 1960. Exterior.*

116.  *Eric Boissonnas House, Cap Bénat, France. Under construction 1962. Model.*

*The Responsibility of the Architect*

There is something that interests me almost as much as architecture itself and that is the moral mainspring of architecture. I don't mean good or bad morals, but the values that we have that lead us to the design. Under what basic living aim do we start doing architecture? I feel that architecture is an art primarily and hardly anything else. I probably go too far in defending this thesis that the aim of architecture is the creation of beautiful spaces, and that everything else is so subordinate to it that it's just as if it didn't exist. . . . This is too practical an age, and all history disproves the idea that architecture is anything but an art. The other point of view, that architecture is a technic, does count today, because of the moral climate of our time. There is no doubt that we believe a great deal in utility as an aim in life, as a good, as a value. But when it gets into architecture, what does this usefulness mean? It means little more than honesty to express the structure. . . .

To me, a purpose is not necessary to make a building beautiful. Naturally we have to have some laboratories that work. In the Middle Ages it wouldn't have been anything, but Wright had to rationalize or [S.C.] Johnson wouldn't have allowed him to build the Tower. It was the terrific problem of a man who wants a beautiful building but the only thing he has to build is a laboratory. Wright puts it into a tower. It doesn't work; it doesn't have to work. Wright had that shape conceived long before he knew what was going into it. I claim that is where architecture starts, with the concept. . . .

There is no search, there is no research, there is a discovery of form either here or in the air. Where form comes from I don't know, but it has nothing at all to do with the sociological aspects of architecture. It does not come from paintings.

(From *Perspecta*, II, 1954, with permission of author and editors.)


*"The Seven Crutches of Modern Architecture"*
(Remarks from an informal talk to students of Architectural Design at Harvard, December 1954)


Art has nothing to do with intellectual pursuit—it shouldn't be in a university at all. Art should be practiced in gutters—pardon me, in attics.

You can't learn architecture any more than you can learn a sense of music or of painting. You shouldn't talk about art, you should do it.

If I seem to go into words it's because there's no other way to communicate. We have to descend to the world around us if we are to battle it. We have to use words to put the "word" people back where they belong.

So I'm going to attack the seven crutches of architecture. Some of us rejoice in the crutches and pretend that we're walking and that poor other people with two feet are slightly handicapped. But we all use them at times, and especially in the schools where you have to use language. It's only natural to use language when you're teaching, because how are teachers to mark you? . . . Schools therefore are especially prone to using these crutches. I would certainly use them if I were teaching, because I couldn't criticize extra-aesthetic props any better than any other teacher.

The most important crutch in recent times is not valid now: the Crutch of History. In the old days you could always rely on books. You could say, "What do you mean you don't like my tower? There it is in Wren." Or, "They did that on the Sub-treasury Building—why can't I do it?" History doesn't bother us very much now.

But the next one is still with us today although, here again, the Crutch of Pretty Drawing is pretty well gone. There are those of us—I am one—who have made sort of a cult of the pretty plan. It's a wonderful crutch because you can give yourself the illusion that you are creating architecture while you're making pretty drawings. Fundamentally, architecture is something you build and put together, and people walk in and they like it. But that's too hard. Pretty pictures are easier.

The next one, the third one, is the Crutch of Utility, of Usefulness. This is where I was brought up, and I've used it myself; it was an old Harvard habit. They say a building is good architecture if it works. Of course, . . . all buildings work. . . . The Parthenon probably worked perfectly well for the ceremonies that they used it for. In other words, merely that a building works is not sufficient. You expect that it works. You expect a kitchen hot water faucet to run hot water these days. You expect any architect . . . to be able to put the kitchen in the right place. But when it's used as a crutch it impedes. It lulls you into thinking that that is architecture. The rules that we've all been brought up on, "The coat closet

should be near the front door in a house," "Cross-ventilation
is a necessity,"—these rules are not very important for architecture. That we should have a front door to come in and a
back door to carry the garbage out—pretty good, but in my
house I noticed to my horror the other day that I carried the
garbage out the front door. If the business of getting the house
to run well takes precedence over your artistic invention the
result won't be architecture at all; merely an assemblage of
useful parts. You will recognize it next time you're doing a
building: you'll be so satisfied when you get the banks of
elevators to come out at the right floor you'll think your
skyscraper is finished. I know. I'm just working on one.

That's not as bad, though, as the next one: the Crutch of
Comfort. That's a habit that we come by, the same as utility.
We are all descended from John Stuart Mill in our thinking.
After all, what is architecture for but the comforts of the
people that live there? But when that is made into a crutch for
doing architecture, environmental control starts to replace
architecture. Pretty soon you'll be doing controlled environmental houses which aren't hard to do except that you may
have a window on the west and you can't control the sun.
There isn't an overhang in the world, there isn't a sun chart in
Harvard University that will help. Because, of course, the sun
is absolutely everywhere. You know what they mean by
controlled environment—it is the study of "microclimatology," which is the science that tells you how to recreate a
climate so that you will be comfortable. But are you? The fireplace, for example, is out of place in the controlled environment of a house. It heats up and throws off thermostats. But
I like the beauty of a fireplace so I keep my thermostat way
down to 60, and then I light a big roaring fire so I can move
back and forth. Now that's not controlled environment. I
control the environment. It's a lot more fun.

Some people say that chairs are good-looking that are comfortable. Are they? I think that comfort is a function of
whether you think the chair is good-looking or not. Just test
it yourself. (Except I know you won't be honest with me.) I
have had Mies van der Rohe chairs now for twenty-five years
in my home wherever I go. They're not very comfortable
chairs, but, if people like the looks of them they say, "Aren't
these beautiful chairs," which indeed they are. Then they'll
sit in them and say, "My, aren't they comfortable." If, however, they're the kind of people who think curving steel legs

are an ugly way to hold up a chair they'll say, "My, what uncomfortable chairs."

The Crutch of Cheapness. That is one that you haven't run into as students because no one's told you to cut $10,000 off the budget because you haven't built anything. But that'll be your first lesson. The cheapness boys will say, "Anybody can build an expensive house. Ah, but see, my house only cost $25,000." Anybody that can build a $25,000 house has indeed reason to be proud, but is he talking about architecture or his economic ability? Is it the crutch you're talking about, or is it architecture? That economic motive, for instance, goes in New York so far that the real estate minded people consider it un-American to build a Lever House with no rentals on the ground floor. They find that it's an architectural sin not to fill the envelope.

Then there's another very bad crutch that you will get much later in your career. Please, please watch out for this one: the Crutch of Serving the Client. You can escape all criticism if you can say, "Well, the client wanted it that way." Mr. Hood, one of our really great architects, talked exactly that way. He would put a Gothic door on a skyscraper and say, "Why shouldn't I? The client wanted a Gothic door on the modern skyscraper, and I put it on. Because what is my business? Am I not here to please my client?" . . . Where do you draw the line? When do the client's demands permit you to shoot him, and when do you give in gracefully? It's got to be clear, back in your own mind, that serving the client is one thing and the art of architecture another.

Perhaps the most trouble of all is the Crutch of Structure. That gets awfully near home because, of course, I use it all the time myself. I'm going to go on using it. You have to use something. Like Bucky Fuller, who's going around from school to school—it's like a hurricane, you can't miss it if it's coming: he talks, you know, for five or six hours, and he ends up that all architecture is nonsense, and you have to build something like discontinuous domes. The arguments are beautiful. I have nothing against discontinuous domes, but for goodness sakes, let's not call it architecture. Have you ever seen Bucky trying to put a door into one of his domed buildings? He's never succeeded, and wisely, when he does them, he doesn't put any covering on them, so they are magnificent pieces of pure sculpture. Sculpture alone cannot result in architecture because architecture has problems that Bucky

Fuller has not faced, like how do you get in and out. Structure
is a very dangerous thing to cling to. You can be led to believe
that clear structure clearly expressed will end up being architecture by itself. You say, "I don't have to design any more.
All I have to do is make a clean structural order." I have
believed this off and on myself. It's a very nice crutch, you
see, because, after all, you can't mess up a building too badly
if the bays are all equal and all the windows the same size.

Now why should we at this stage be that crutch conscious?
Why should we not step right up to it and face it? That act of
creation. The act of creation, like birth and death, you have
to face by yourself. There aren't any rules; there is no one to
tell you whether your one choice out of, say, six billion for
the proportion of a window is going to be right. No one can
go with you into that room where you make the final decision.
You can't escape it anyhow; why fight it? Why not realize that
architecture is the sum of inescapable artistic decisions that
you have to make. If you're strong you can make them.

I like the thought that what we are to do on this earth is to
embellish it for its greater beauty, so that oncoming generations can look back to the shapes we leave here and get the
same thrill that I get in looking back at theirs—at the Parthenon, at Chartres Cathedral. That is the duty—I doubt if I
get around to it in my generation—the difficulties are too
many, but you can. You can if you're strong enough not to
bother with the crutches, and face the fact that to create something is a direct experience.

I like Corbusier's definition of architecture. He expressed
it the way I wish I could have: *"L'architecture, c'est le jeux,
savant, correct et magnifique, des formes sous la lumière"*—
"Architecture is the play of forms under the light, the play
of forms correct, wise, magnificent." The play of forms under
the light. And, my friends, that's all it is. . . . I like Nietzsche's definition—that much-misunderstood European—he
said, "In architectural works, man's pride, man's triumph
over gravitation, man's will to power assume visible form.
Architecture is a veritable oratory of power made by form."

Now my position in all this is obviously not as solipsistic,
not as directly intuitional as all that sounds. To get back to
earth, what do we do next? If we don't hang on to any of
these crutches. I'm a traditionalist. I believe in history. I mean
by tradition the carrying out, in freedom, the development of a
certain basic approach to architecture which we find upon

118 beginning our work here. I do not believe in perpetual revolution in architecture. I do not strive for originality. As Mies once told me, "Philip, it is much better to be good than to be original." I believe that. We have very fortunately the work of our spiritual fathers to build on. We hate them, of course, as all spiritual sons hate all spiritual fathers, but we can't ignore them, nor can we deny their greatness. The men, of course, that I refer to: Walter Gropius, Le Corbusier and Mies van der Rohe. Frank Lloyd Wright I should include—the greatest architect of the nineteenth century. Isn't it wonderful to have behind us the tradition, the work that those men have done? Can you imagine being alive at a more wonderful time? Never in history was the tradition so clearly demarked, never were the great men so great, never could we learn so much from them and go our own way, without feeling constricted by any style, and knowing that what we do is going to be the architecture of the future, and not be afraid that we wander into some little bypath, like today's romanticists, where nothing can possibly evolve. In that sense I am a traditionalist.

(From *Perspecta*, III, 1955, with permission of the author and the editors.)

### Where Are We At?

Architecture, one would think, has its own validity. It needs no reference to any other discipline to make it "viable" or to "justify" its value. We might even question whether words like value or morals are applicable to an architectural style. The International Style, for example, needs no one to say it was good or it was bad. Greek and Gothic styles were loved and reviled throughout subsequent ages and neither opinion affected the architecture itself, but were comments rather on the state of mind of the lover or the reviler. The International Style is its own justification. We can dislike it, which most of us may today, but we are obviously much too close to have any interesting views on its future influence or its position in the history books.

For the sake of the argument let us admit that we do live in a machine age. We can hardly call to question an architectural style that evolved in that age for not expressing it. The International Style "expressed its age" merely by the fact of being prevalent at that time.

(From *The Architectural Review*, September, 1960, with permission of the author and the editors.)

The phrase "International Style" has had a varied career. Accepted by some historians, reviled by Giedion and most architects, perhaps a majority of you here tonight.

. . . It might be well therefore to preface my remarks with a word of explanation of what the phrase means to its inventors. Alfred Barr and Russell Hitchcock used the phrase first in 1931 when we were all searching for a name for the obviously clear line of work being done in the '20's by men like Le Corbusier, Mies, and Gropius. It was obvious it was a style. It was obviously different from the individualist work of before the war. That the practitioners of it at the time did not consider it a style was only natural. None of us architects want to feel we are working in straitjackets. But it is nevertheless the duty of the historian to point out styles when they occur in history. . . .

I recognize three quite interesting ways of doing architecture in the past decade, intertwined, none of them a style, but all exhilarating, forward looking, fecund, I would say, for future forms.

The one line is still the International Style. Mies is by no means through creating. . . . Let us not write off the grand, modern 40-year tradition. After all who wants the job of doing New York's next all-out skyscraper. . . .

The second great stream I recognize is what the British sometimes call Brutalist. Not a good name, but nevertheless a name. It is an attitude, not an architecture, stemming from a neo-functionalist approach to building. Not clarity of expression, but fulfillment of environmental purpose is now the word. As forms the Brutalists are apt to bring us great concrete beams and scattered windows in brick, with much in and out. This is functional variety. Formalistically, since, in my opinion, forms always follow forms and not function, their designs are apt to be taken from the Jaoul Houses by Le Corbusier. The regular skeletal rhythms of the International Style are gone. . . .

This Brutalist attitude melts on into another very popular direction; we can go back to the British once again for its name, Neo-Historicism. To many this movement is a slap at the Modern Movement as a whole and its sociological functional background. But it is not.

120  Let us take America's most impressive new building: Lou Kahn's Medical Research Building in Philadelphia. It is very much a functionalist building. Lou made careful studies of exhaust hoods and the paraphernalia of laboratories. He made a careful study of exposed structure. But he went beyond, and who can doubt that the towers of San Gimignano were present in his mind?

You see what a very different usage of history this is from the Revivalist or Eclectic architecture of the 19th century. This is a free wheeling, allusive, far fetched adaptation. This attitude to history is also opposite to the mechanistic denial of history by the pure functionalists of the '20's or of today. We find ourselves now all wrapped up in reminiscence. We cannot not know history. The English and Italians are apt to look back a shorter period than are we: to *de Stijl*, or late Corbu, for example, but in essence, the new view of history is a new and stimulating impulse. We no longer have to judge buildings by how much or how little history they adopt, hating all reminiscence, but rather how well they have adopted. Yamasaki's Gothic tracery in Seattle, Saarinen's medieval village at Yale, or Gropius's Moslem University. How well have they done? . . .

(Unpublished notes, March 30, 1961.)


*Letter to Dr. Jurgen Joedicke*

I am very much impressed by your summation of modern international architecture in 1961. Your sense of organization and characterization in a field as fluid as ours is clear and consistent . . .

Two points I should like to bring out. First, I wish you had the time to study American architecture more at first hand. The architects best known to European colleagues and journalists are the ones you especially discuss. To us Schindler might be singled out instead of Neutra—Kahn instead of Breuer and so forth. Also in talks perhaps we could make clear the differences between Stone, Yamasaki and myself.

May I say parenthetically, you are very fair with me. Borromini should not be mentioned in connection with my work. The New Harmony shrine is pure form—ugly or beautiful—but pure form.

There is, as you realize, however, a basic cleavage in our points of view. You criticize from a standpoint (Standpunkt). You take a stand (Stellung nehmen), on a moral basis of the Modern Movement. You understand the modern movement as deriving "Form" from the proper program (Aufgabe) and from structural simplicity and honesty. You take especial stand against using structure shapes as mere applied decoration. You would agree with Goethe: "Der Pilaster is eine Lüge."

In line with this, you naturally would see the danger of a new Eclecticism in our new approach to history.

Is there not, however, another position we could take? Namely, that the entire modern movement—looked at as an intellectual movement dating from Ruskin and Viollet-le-Duc, going through the Werkbund, Bauhaus, Le Corbusier to World War II—may be winding up its days.

There is only one absolute today and that is change. There are no rules, surely no certainties in any of the arts. There is only the feeling of a wonderful freedom, of endless possibilities to investigate, of endless past years of historically great buildings to enjoy.

I cannot worry about a new eclecticism. Even Richardson who considered himself an eclectic was not one. A good architect will always do original work. A bad one would do bad "modern" work as well as bad work (that is imitative) with historical forms.

Structural honesty seems to me one of the bugaboos that we should free ourselves from very quickly. The Greeks with their marble columns imitating wood, and covering up the wood roofs inside! The Gothic designers with their wooden roofs above to protect their delicate vaulting. And Michelangelo, the greatest architect in history, with his Mannerist column!

No, our day no longer has need of moral crutches of late 19th century vintage. If Viollet-le-Duc was what the young Frank Lloyd Wright was nurtured on, Geoffrey Scott and Russell Hitchcock were my Bibles.

I am old enough to have enjoyed the International Style immensely and worked in it with the greatest pleasure. I still believe Le Corbusier and Mies to be the greatest living architects. But now the age is changing so fast. Old values are

122  swept away by new with dizzying but thrilling speed. Long live Change!

The danger you see of a sterile academic eclecticism is no danger. The danger is the opposite, the sterility of your Academy of the Modern Movement.

(Letter of December 6, 1961, to Dr. Joedicke, historian and critic of contemporary architecture.)

SIGNIFICANT WRITINGS BY PHILIP JOHNSON

"Rejected Architects," *Creative Art*, VIII, June, 1931, pp. 433–35.

*The International Style: Architecture Since 1922* (in collaboration with Henry-Russell Hitchcock), with an introduction by Alfred H. Barr, New York, 1932.

*Modern Architects*, exhibition catalogue, Museum of Modern Art, New York (in collaboration with Alfred H. Barr, Henry-Russell Hitchcock and Lewis Mumford), New York, 1932. (Johnson contributed to the introduction and wrote the sections on Mies van der Rohe and Otto Haesler.)

"Decorative Art a Generation Ago," *Creative Art*, XII, April, 1933, pp. 297–99. (An early plea in favor of Art Nouveau.)

"Mies van der Rohe," *Architectural Record*, CII, September, 1947, pp. 81–88.

*Mies van der Rohe*, New York, Museum of Modern Art, 1947. New edition, with an additional chapter, 1953.

"Architectural Freedom and Order: An Answer to Robert W. Kennedy," *Magazine of Art*, XLI, October, 1948, pp. 228–31 (in collaboration with Peter Blake).

"The Buildings We See," *New World Writing*, Vol. 1, April, 1952, pp. 109–30 (in collaboration with Henry-Russell Hitchcock).

"On the Responsibility of the Architect," discussion with Louis Kahn, Vincent Scully, Pietro Belluschi, and Paul Weiss, *Perspecta, The Yale Architectural Journal*, II, 1954, pp. 45–57.

"Correct and Magnificent Play," *Art News*, LII, September, 1953, pp. 16, 52–53. (Review of Le Corbusier, *Oeuvre Complète*, Vol. V.)

"School at Hunstanton," *Architectural Review*, CXVI, No. 634, September, 1954, p. 148. (Commentary on the Miesian aspect of the now-famous building by A. & P. Smithson.)

"The Seven Crutches of Modern Architecture," *Perspecta, The Yale Architectural Journal*, III, 1955, pp. 40–44.

"The Wiley House," *Perspecta, The Yale Architectural Journal*, III, 1955, p. 45. (Commentary on one of his major houses.)

"Is Sullivan the Father of Functionalism," *Art News*, LV, December, 1956, pp. 44–46. (Unusual and personal reaction to Sullivan's role in Modern Architecture; surprisingly negative tone.)

"Conversations Regarding the Future of Architecture" (excerpts from record distributed by Reynolds Metal Co.), *Print*, II, February–March, 1957, pp. 37–38.

"100 Years, Frank Lloyd Wright and Us," *Pacific Architect and Builder*, March, 1957, pp. 13, 35–36.

"Parthenon, Perfection and All That," *Art News*, LVIII, March, 1959, p. 43. (A review of A. W. Lawrence, *Greek Architecture*.)

"Letter to the Museum Director," *Museum News*, January, 1960, pp. 22–25.

"Three Architects," *Art in America*, XLVIII, No. 1, Spring, 1960, pp. 70–75. (Notes on Louis Kahn, Paul Rudolph, and F. Kiesler.)

"Where Are We At?" *The Architectural Review*, CXXVIII, No. 763, September, 1960, pp. 173–75. (Review of Henry-Russell Hitchcock, *Architecture, Nineteenth and Twentieth Centuries* and Reyner Banham, *Theory and Design in the First Machine Age.*)

"Architectural Student Jonathan Barnett Interviews Architect Philip Johnson," *Architectural Record*, CXXVIII, No. 6, December, 1960, p. 16.

"Nine Actual Theater Designs," *Musical America*, January, 1961, annual issue.

"Johnson," *Perspecta, The Yale Architectural Journal*, VII, 1961, pp. 3–8.

## SIGNIFICANT WRITINGS ABOUT PHILIP JOHNSON

(Note: only those magazine articles of a critical intent are noted here; mere illustrative presentations in the professional press have been excluded. The interested reader will find such material listed in the *Art Index.*)

Hitchcock, Henry-Russell and Drexler, Arthur, *Built in U.S.A.: Post-War Architecture*, New York, 1953, (with a preface by Philip Johnson), pp. 35–36; 72–75.

Hitchcock, Henry-Russell, "Philip Johnson," *The Architectural Review*, CXVII, April, 1955, pp. 236–47.

Hitchcock, Henry-Russell, *Architecture, Nineteenth and Twentieth Centuries*, Harmondsworth and Baltimore, 1958, pp. 380, 389, 423–25.

Hitchcock, Henry-Russell, "Current Work of Philip Johnson," *Zodiac*, VIII, 1961, pp. 64–81.

"House at New Canaan, Connecticut, Architect: Philip Johnson," *The Architectural Review*, CVIII, No. 645, September, 1950, pp. 152–60. (Complete visual presentation of the Glass House, completed in 1949, together with comparative illustrations and the architect's own comments concerning his sources of inspiration.)

Jordy, W. H., "Seagram Assessed," *The Architectural Review*, CXXIV, December, 1958, pp. 374–82.

Jordy, W. H., "Mies-less Johnson," *Architectural Forum*, CXI, September, 1959, pp. 114–23.

Jordy, W. H., "Formal Image U.S.A.," *The Architectural Review*, CXXVII, March, 1960, pp. 157–65.

McCallum, Ian, *Architecture U.S.A.*, London and New York, 1959, pp. 116–24.

Scully, Vincent, Jr., "Archetype and Order in Recent American Architecture," *Art in America*, XLII, December, 1954, pp. 253–57.

Scully, Vincent, Jr., *Modern Architecture, the Architecture of Democracy*, New York, 1961.

Numbers in regular roman type refer to text pages; *italic* figures refer to the plates.

Altes Museum, Berlin (Schinkel), 40, *89B*
Amon Carter Museum of Western Art, Fort Worth, Tex., 23, 39, 40, 41, *84–88*
*Architectural Review, The,* 14
Armour Institute, Chicago, 21
Asia House, New York City, 41, *100–102*

Ball House, New Canaan, Conn., 23, *33*
Barcelona Pavilion (Mies), 24, 31, 37
Baroque, 17, 27, 38
Barr, Alfred, 119
Bauhaus, Dessau (Gropius), 11, 12, 13, 24, 121
Bay Region Style, 14
Boissonnas (Eric) House I, New Canaan, Conn., 16, 23, 28, 29, 32, 33, 34, 35, *58–62*
Boissonnas House II, Cap Bénat, France, *116*
Booth House project, 30
Borromini, Francesco, 121
Breuer, Marcel, 13, 14, 29, 121
Bronxville, New York: Sarah Lawrence College, 42, 43, *115*
Brown University, Computing Laboratory, Providence, R.I., 42, *113*
Brutalist, 119, 120
Burden (William A. M.) House, project for, Mt. Kisco, N.Y., 28, *55–57*
Burlington, Lord (Richard Boyle), 18

Cambridge, Massachusetts: Johnson House, 25, 27, *1, 2*
Chandigarh: High Court Building (Le Corbusier), 40, *89A*
Charlottesville, Virginia: University of Virginia, 36, *71A*
Chicago, Illinois: Convention Hall, projects for (Mies), 28; Evans House (Wright), 32; Illinois Institute of Technology (Mies), 14, 21, 35, 36, *71B*
Computing Laboratory, Brown University, Providence, R.I., 42, *113*
*Constructivism* (Russia), 12
Costa, Lúcio, 13
Cullinan Wing, Museum of Fine Arts, Houston, Tex. (Mies), 37, *73*

Davis (Richard) House, Wayzata, Ill., 29, 31, 34, 37, *43–47*

De Mondrot House, Le Pradet (Le Corbusier), 30
Dessau, Germany: Bauhaus (Gropius), 11, 12, 13, 24
*De Stijl* (Holland), 12, 120

Eclecticism, 17, 120, 121, 122
Evans House, Chicago (Wright), 32

Farney House, Sagaponack, Long Island, N.Y., 29, *3, 4*
Farnsworth House, Plano, Ill. (Mies), 23, 25, 26, 30, 32, *14*
Fort Worth, Texas: Amon Carter Museum of Western Art, 23, 39, 40, 41, *84–88*
Four Seasons Restaurant, Seagram Building, New York City, *98, 99*
Fuller, Buckminster, 116, 117
*Futurism* (Italy), 12

Gabriel, Jacques-Ange, 18
Germanic Romantic Classicism, 38
Giedion, Sigfried, 119
Glass House, New Canaan, Conn., 15, 17, 22–27, 28, 29, 30, 31, 32, 33, 36, *5–13; 15–17* (see Johnson Residence)
Goethe, Johann Wolfgang von, 121
Gropius, Walter, 11, 12, 13, 21, 118, 119, 120; Bauhaus, Dessau, 11, 12, 13, 24, 121
Guest House, New Canaan, Conn., 26, 28, 30, 36, *6, 7* (see Glass House)
Guggenheim Museum, New York City (Wright), 18, 38, *75*

Harvard Graduate School of Design, 21
High Court Building, Chandigarh (Le Corbusier), 40, *89A*
Hitchcock, Henry-Russell, co-author (with Philip Johnson) of *The International Style,* 12, 20, 26, 119, 122
Hodgson (Richard) House, New Canaan, Conn., 29, 30, 31, 34, *25–28*
Houston, Texas: Museum of Fine Arts, Cullinan Wing (Mies), 37, *73;* University of St. Thomas, 35, 36, *68–70*
Howe, George, 13

Illinois Institute of Technology (Mies), Chicago, 14, 21, 35, 36, *71B*
Industrial Classicism, 36

126   International Style, 11, 12, 13, 14, 17, 19, 20, 22, 24, 25, 118, 119, 120, 122
"International Style—Death or Metamorphosis," 119–120
*International Style, The,* 12
Irvington, New York: Oneto (George) House, 29, 30, *21–24*

Jaoul Houses (Le Corbusier), 120
Jefferson, Thomas, 36, *71A*
Joedicke, Dr. Jurgen, 120, 122
Johnson (Philip) House, Cambridge, Mass., 25, 27, *1, 2;* Pavilion, New Canaan, Conn., *103;* Residence, New Canaan, 13, 15, 22, 23, 24, 25, 26, 27, 28, 29, 30, 31, 32, 33, 36, *5–13, 15–17*
Johnson, Philip, literary works of: biography, *Mies van der Rohe,* 15; co-author (with Henry-Russell Hitchcock) of *The International Style,* 12

Kahn, Louis I., 13, 16, 18, 21, 120, 121; Medical Research Bldg., Philadelphia, Penn., 120
Kent, William, 18
Kline Science Tower, Yale University, New Haven, Conn., *114*
Kneses Tifereth Israel Synagogue, Port Chester, N.Y., 34, 35, 39, *63–66*
Kootz Gallery Exhibit, 1951, house project for, *16*

Le Corbusier, 12, 13, 14, 15, 22, 30, 40, 42, 118, 119, 120, 121, 122; de Mondrot House, Le Pradet, 30; definition of architecture, 117; High Court Building, Chandigarh, 40, *89A;* Jaoul Houses, 120; *Unité d'Habitation,* Marseilles, 14; Villa Savoye, Poissy, 30, *38*
Ledoux, Claude-Nicolas, 22
Leonhardt (Robert) House, Lloyd's Neck, Long Island, N.Y., 23, 29, 31, 32, *50–54*
Letter to Dr. Jurgen Joedicke, 120–122
Lincoln Center, New York State Theater, 35, 40, 41, 43, *92–97*
Lincoln, Nebraska: Sheldon Art Gallery, University of Nebraska, 23, 40, *90, 91*
Lipchitz, Jacques, sculpture, 41
Lloyd's Neck, Long Island, N.Y.: Leonhardt (Robert) House, 23, 29, 31, 32, *50–54*
Lurçat, André, 12

Malevich, Kasimir, 22
Mannerist column, 122
Marin County Center, California (Wright), 18
Marseilles, France: *Unité d'Habitation* (Le Corbusier), 14

Medical Research Building, Philadelphia, Penn. (Kahn), 120
"Mesopotamian," 42
Michelangelo, 121, 122
"Microclimatology," 115
Mies van der Rohe, Ludwig, 11, 12, 13, 14, 15, 18, 21, 22, 29, 33, 35, 118, 119, 122; Barcelona Pavilion, 24, 31, 37; chairs, 116; Chicago Convention Hall, projects for, 28; Cullinan Wing, Museum of Fine Arts, Houston, Tex., 39, *73;* Farnsworth House, Plano, Ill., 23, 25, 26, 30, 32, *14;* Illinois Institute of Technology, Chicago, 14, 21, 35, 36, *71B;* Industrial Classicism, 36; museum designs, 37; Museum for a Small City of 1942, project for, 37; Museum of Fine Arts, Cullinan Wing, Houston, Tex., 37, 71; Reichsbank project, 27; Seagram Building, New York City (in collaboration with Johnson), 17, *98, 99*
Mill, John Stuart, 115
Modern Movement, 120, 121, 122
Mt. Kisco, New York: Burden (William A. M.) House, project for, 28, *55–57*
Munson - Williams - Proctor Institute, Utica, N.Y., 16, 23, 31, 36, 37, 38, 40, 43, *72, 74, 76–83*
Museum of Modern Art, Annex, New York, 41, *67;* Sculpture Court, 27, 28, 42, *39–42*
Museum for a Small City of 1942, project for (Mies), 37

Neo-Historicism, 120
Neo-International Style, 25
*Neo-Picturesque,* 14
Neutra, Richard, 13, 121
New Canaan, Connecticut: Ball (Alice) House, 23, *33;* Boissonnas (Eric) House, 16, 23, 28, 29, 32, 33, 34, 35, *58–62;* Glass House (Johnson), 13, 15, 22, 23, 24, 25, 26, 27, 28, 29, 30, 31, 32, 33, 36, *5–13; 15–17;* Glass Pavilion (Johnson), 25, *103;* Guest House (Johnson), 26, 28, 30, 36, *6, 7;* Hodgson (Richard) House, 29, 30, 31, 34, *25–28;* Wiley (Robert) House, 23, 29, 30, 31, *34–37;* House for Wiley Development Company, 23, *48, 49*
*New Empiricism* (Scandinavia), 14
New Harmony, Indiana: Roofless Church, 27, 41, 42, 43, 121, *104–107*
New York City: Asia House, 41, *100–102;* Guggenheim Museum, 18, 38, *75;* Museum of Modern Art Annex, 41, *67;* New York State Theater,

Lincoln Center, 35, 40, 41, 43, *92–97*; Rockefeller Guest House, 27, 28, *18–20*; Seagram Building (Mies-Johnson), 17, *98, 99*; Sculpture Court, Museum of Modern Art, 27, 28, 42, *39–42*

Niemeyer, Oscar, 13

Nietzsche, Friedrich, definition of architecture by, 117, 118

Nuclear Reactor, Rehovot, Israel, 23, 35, 41, 42, 43, *108–112*

Oak Park Unity Temple (Wright), 38

Oneto (George) House, Irvington, N.Y., 29, 30, *21–24*

Oud, J. J. P., 12

Palladian, 26, 27, 29

Poissy, France: Villa Savoye (Le Corbusier), 30, *38*

Port Chester, New York: Kneses Tifereth Israel Synagogue, 34, 35, 39, *63–66*

Post-Baroque, 38

Post-International Style, 13

Potsdam villas (Schinkel), 29

Prairie Style (Wright), 32, 33

Providence, Rhode Island: Computing Laboratory, Brown University, 42, *113*

*Purism* (France), 12

Rehovot, Israel: Nuclear Reactor, 23, 35, 41, 42, 43, *108–112*

Reichsbank project (Mies), 27

Reidy, Affonso Eduardo, 13

"Responsibility of the Architect," 113

Revivalism, 17, 120

Richardson, Henry Hobson, 19, 20, 121

Ridgefield, Connecticut: Schlumberger Administration Building, 34, *29–32*

Rietveld, Gerrit, 12

Rockefeller Guest House, New York City, 27, 28, *18–20*

Romantic Classicism, 22, 36, 39

Roofless Church, New Harmony, Ind., 27, 41, 42, 43, 121, *104–107*

Rudolph, Paul, 13, 16, 18

Ruskin, John, 121

Saarinen, Eero, 13, 16, 18, 42, 120

Sagaponack, Long Island, N.Y., Farney House, 29, *3, 4*

Sarah Lawrence College, Bronxville, N.Y., 42, 43, *115*

Schindler, Rudolph, 13, 121

Schinkel, Karl Friedrich, 22, 29, 32, 33, 35, 39; Altes Museum, Berlin, 40, *89B*; Potsdam villas, 29

Schlumberger Administration Bldg., Ridgefield, Conn., 34, *29–32*

Scott, Geoffery, 122

Sculpture Court, Museum of Modern Art, New York City, 27, 28, *39–42*

Seagram Building, New York City (Mies-Johnson), 17, *98, 99*

"Seven Crutches of Modern Architecture," 114–118

Sheldon Art Gallery, University of Nebraska, Lincoln, Neb., 23, 40, *90, 91*

Soane, Sir John, 35, 39

Stone, Edward, 18, 121

Sullivan, Louis, 19, 20

*Unité d'Habitation*, Marseilles (Le Corbusier), 14

University of Nebraska, Sheldon Art Gallery, Lincoln, Neb., 23, 40, *90, 91*

University of St. Thomas, Houston, Tex., 35, 36, *68–70*

University of Virginia, Charlottesville, Va. (Jefferson), 36, *71A*

Utica, New York: Munson-Williams-Proctor Institute, 16, 23, 31, 36, 37, 38, 40, 43, *72, 74, 76–83*

Van Doesburg, Theo, 22

Villa Savoye, Poissy, France (Le Corbusier), 30, *38*

Viollet-le-Duc, 121, 122

Wayzata, Minnesota: Davis (Richard) House, 29, 31, 34, 37, *43–47*

"Where Are We At?" 118–119

Wiley (Robert) House, New Canaan, Conn., 23, 29, 30, 31, *34–37*

Wiley Development Company, House for, New Canaan, Conn., 23, *48, 49*

Wren, Sir Christopher, 114

Wright, Frank Lloyd, 18, 19, 20, 21, 32, 33, 39, 42, 113, 118, 122; Evans House, Chicago, 34; Guggenheim Museum, New York City, 18, 38, *75*; Marin County Center, Calif., 18; Oak Park Unity Temple, 38; Prairie Style, 32, 33

Yale University, New Haven, Conn., Kline Science Tower, *114*

Yamasaki, Minoru, 13, 120, 121

All the photographs of Johnson's work were supplied through the courtesy of Philip Johnson Associates with the permission of the photographers.

Text printed in offset by Murray Printing Company, Forge Village, Massachusetts; illustrations in Pictone offset by Pictorial Offset, New York City. Set in Bodoni Book with Inserat Grotesk. Bound by The Haddon Craftsmen, Scranton, Pennsylvania. Format by Lustig & Reich.